Movements in American History

by Ann Lockledge

illustrated by Don Ellens

cover illustration by Rick Clubb

Publisher
Instructional Fair • TS Denison
Grand Rapids, Michigan 49544

ISBN: 1-56822-438-9
Movements in American History
Copyright © 1997 by Instructional Fair • TS Denison
2400 Turner Avenue NW
Grand Rapids, Michigan 49544

Table of Contents

Introduction

The theme of movements is an approach to teaching history that looks at what is happening in the United States during a particular era and provides interesting and creative approaches to the events rather than merely jumping from war to war.

Students need materials that will encourage them to finish meaningful assignments without coercion or teacher intervention. It is the purpose of this book to provide instructional materials that will motivate students to think and take responsibility for their own learning. These activities give direction and purpose to learning about American history by offering the kinds of choices that promote perseverance.

The first page in each section is intended as a student information page that might serve as either a cognitive organizer before the lesson or a summary statement after lectures are completed. An assumption is made that a textbook is available, but it is also recognized that many students cannot read textbooks on their own. One way to use this page would be for the teacher to read the page as students follow, so that they pick up on inflections and proper pronunciation. The students then put aside the reading and rewrite the ideas the best they can from their memory. After this, a few students are asked to read their comments aloud. Students discuss with the teacher or in small groups what they might want to include in these comments. At this point, they might decide to add additional details or to change the wording.

The "Just for Teachers" pages are designed to go into greater depth for the teacher. Additional background is included so that the materials in that section will fit more closely into an overall plan. An explanation of each of the student activity pages is given so that you, the teacher, can see how it fits in with what is being taught. Sufficient directions are also given on the student pages so that, if necessary, the sheet could be handed to a student without additional explanation. This makes the sheets useful in a contract, a center, or for the student who has been absent.

Each of the student pages is labeled with a bubble telling the type of strategy that is being used. This is for the benefit of both teacher and student. It makes it easier for the teacher to ensure that a variety of different learning styles are being addressed. It also helps answer the perennial student question, "Why am I doing this?" When the student realizes the tie between the current activity and learning how to learn, the work becomes more meaningful.

The Explorers Move Out

Curiosity is a great motivator. Europeans, by the end of the 1400s, were curious about the rest of the world in which they lived.

Money is also a great motivator; the Europeans were interested in trading with East Asia, where goods that were in short supply in Europe were plentiful. Because there was no refrigeration, spices like pepper, cinnamon, ginger, and cloves were in great demand to help preserve and flavor food. In search of these spices, Marco Polo and his son had made the difficult overland trip to China and written about their adventures. The Portuguese had found a terrifying route to India by sailing around the Cape of Good Hope at the tip of Africa. It seemed like there must be a better way to reach East Asia.

Christopher Columbus, an Italian navigator, argued that a ship could reach Asia by sailing west about 2,400 miles. He was certain that the world was round and estimated that the ocean voyage west would be shorter than sailing all the way around Africa. Had he known that it was actually three times farther from Spain to China than he thought, he might never have set sail.

Columbus looked everywhere for someone who would back his voyage financially. Finally, Queen Isabella of Spain decided against her advisors and supplied a small fleet of three ships. It was not an easy trip. After a month, the sailors became bored and frightened, but they did not meet up with sea monsters or fall off the edge of the world. At two o'clock on the morning October 12, 1492, a lookout saw a white cliff shining in the moonlight. The expedition had reached an island which Columbus named San Salvador—an island which he assumed was off the coast of China.

When Columbus returned to Spain, he made the new lands sound like the China of Marco Polo. He spoke of rich land and good harbors. Even though the only gold he saw consisted of a few pieces of jewelry worn by the people he called *Indians*, that did not stop him. Besides gold, he said there were spices, cotton plants, beautiful woods, and "a thousand other things of value." Columbus also described new foods such as sweet potatoes and corn that Europeans had never heard of before.

Just for Teachers

Background Information

The price of progress is change and the changes that began with the encounter of 1492 have had a profound impact on the world. Some of these changes may be seen as progress—some may not—but the changes have most certainly resulted in the interdependent world in which we now live. There have been changes in populations, transportation (necessitated by demand for resources and vegetation), government structure, customs, and national boundaries.

It has been said that we can change the world only by changing people, but in fact many changes have been brought about just by changing what mankind eats. The hands-on activity looks at the new and different food that became available to various parts of the world when the Western Hemisphere was opened to European exploration.

Geometrical shapes may be used to organize information. Pyramids may be used to condense information, review facts, follow directions, learn rules, play games, and allow for hands-on learning. Using geometrical shapes is not done to increase information about mathematics but to promote organization. This process of construction will motivate students to study the material. Final products should be displayed.

Student pages

Focus on Research | *Probing for Connections*

On this page, students begin expanding their knowledge about the period of exploration and discovery by finding answers to specific questions. To understand that explorers depended on the instruments and maps that were available at the time, students can research information in books and on computers to develop their own store of data.

Focus on Skills | *The Explorers Keep Coming*

Going from textual material to a graphic representation is an important organizational skill. On this activity page, students merely rearrange the facts from a single sentence. They should then be ready to look through books or other textual material to add to their charts.

Focus on Maps | *More Than One Trip*

The Western Hemisphere was not all discovered in one trip. There were many voyages, made for a variety of reasons. The extent of these travels is best displayed on a map. Using different colors for different voyages and labeling with names and dates will help students have a more complete picture of the era.

Focus on Writing | *Columbus Returns*

Students should first look at the front page of a newspaper and read the headline and the first few sentences of different articles. They will be able to see that the headline is the attention-getter and the first few sentences usually tell who, what, when, where, and why or how. Then, they should be able to construct their own news articles.

Hands-On Activity | *New World—New Foods*

Cut out the information paragraphs from the "New World—New Foods" activity pages and glue each onto a separate card. You may also wish to glue a copy of the directions for making a pyramid on the back of each card. Each group will use a different card. If you do not wish to use groups, duplicate the paragraphs so there are enough for each student to draw a card from a hat.

Each student should construct one triangular pyramid or tetrahedron to illustrate the importance of one food that traveled the world as a result of the Columbian Encounter of 1492. On each face of the pyramid, the student is to write or draw one thing about the food on the card selected. One face will have the name of the food and a picture. Another face is to show the importance of the food at some time in history. The third face will show what caused the food to move and the fourth a popular use of the food today. The figure should be cut out and information placed on the faces before the pyramid is glued together.

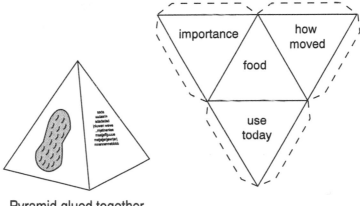

Pyramid glued together

Each section in this book will end with a page of ovals for students to cut out, fill in with an illustration, and assemble into a time line. The ovals can be glued onto connected strips of paper and made into a fan-fold booklet. To use all of the ovals throughout this book, students need to cut five pieces of colored paper lengthwise and glue the pieces into a long strip. The strip is then folded fan style every 3½ inches. Ovals are pasted on each page going along the front and then the back.

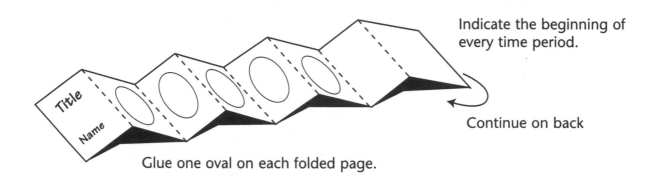

Indicate the beginning of every time period.

Continue on back

Glue one oval on each folded page.

It is not necessary to make one continuous time line from 1492 to the present day. You can have students make time lines of only one era. Once one oval is cut out, it can be traced on plain paper and more ovals added to cover other events or people.

You may wish to divide the class into groups and assign each a specific kind of time line. Possible group assignments would include cultural arts, government and politics, business and the economy, people and their homes, communication and transportation, changes in technology, military involvement, dress and fashion, inventors and inventions, and concerns and issues.

Probing for Connections

When Europeans first came to this continent, they depended on the instruments and maps that were available at the time. Later, explorers had more accurate information to guide them. We can research information today because of the observations and records kept by people throughout history. Using books and computers, see if you can develop your own store of data.

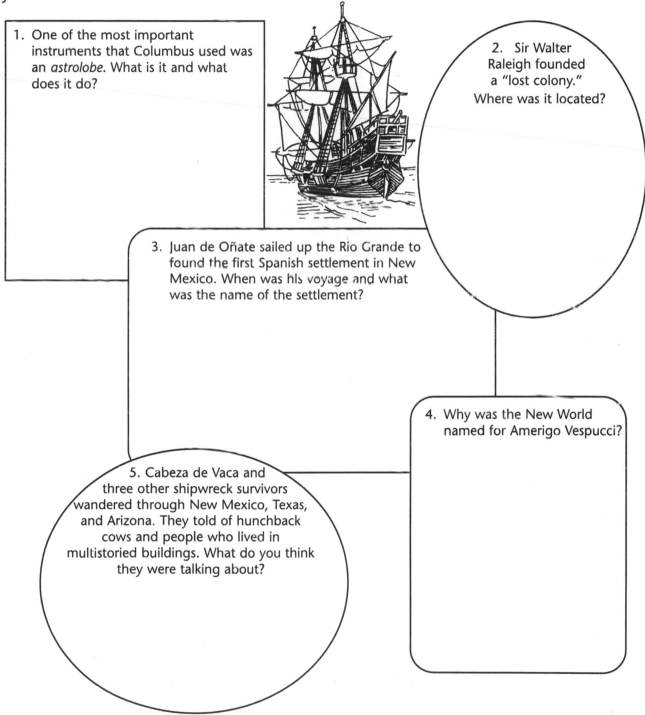

1. One of the most important instruments that Columbus used was an *astrolobe*. What is it and what does it do?

2. Sir Walter Raleigh founded a "lost colony." Where was it located?

3. Juan de Oñate sailed up the Rio Grande to found the first Spanish settlement in New Mexico. When was his voyage and what was the name of the settlement?

4. Why was the New World named for Amerigo Vespucci?

5. Cabeza de Vaca and three other shipwreck survivors wandered through New Mexico, Texas, and Arizona. They told of hunchback cows and people who lived in multistoried buildings. What do you think they were talking about?

Name _____

The Explorers Keep Coming

Use the data contained in the sentences and rearrange it into a chart format. You can then add to your chart by retrieving (finding and using) information about other explorers from your textbook or other sources.

In 1497, John Cabot set sail from England to explore the coast of North America in hopes of setting up trading posts.

During two voyages from 1499 to 1502, Portuguese explorer Amerigo Vespucci traveled along the coast of South America and identified it as a continent.

From 1513 to 1521, Spain's Juan Ponce de León explored Florida, hoping to find gold and the Fountain of Youth.

Giovanni da Verrazano left France in 1524, hoping to find a route to Asia through North America.

Hernando de Soto sailed for Spain from 1539 to 1542 to find gold and to colonize Florida and the Southeast.

From 1540 to 1542, Francisco Vásquez de Coronado explored the Southwest in search of gold and the Seven Cities of Cibola for Spain, only to discover the Grand Canyon.

Sieur Robert Cavelier de La Salle made many trips for France from 1669 to 1682 from the Great Lakes to the lower Mississippi.

Data Retrieval Chart

Explorer	Date	From	Achievement Desired

More Than One Trip

On the map below, trace the voyages of at least five explorers who came to the New World in the 150 years between 1492 and 1642.

Columbus Returns

You are a newspaper editor who is planning the front page of the paper for the day that Columbus arrived back in Spain after his first voyage. The first thing you have to do is decide on the headline and first paragraph of the lead article.

Banner Headline

As you begin to write, remember that the first few sentences of newspaper articles always tell who, what, when, where, and why or how.

First Paragraph of Lead Article

_____

_____

_____

_____

_____

_____

_____

_____

_____

_____

_____

_____

_____

_____

_____

New World—New Foods

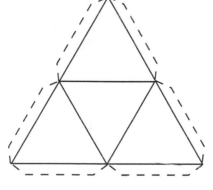

Cut out large triangle.

Trace four triangles in this pattern on construction paper.

Draw on glue tabs.

Cut out the pyramid.

Fold toward center on every line.

You will be making a triangular pyramid to illustrate the importance of the food that traveled the world as a result of the Columbian Encounter of 1492. On the base of your pyramid, write your name and the name of your food. On the other three faces, illustrate 1) the importance of the food, 2) the movement of the food, 3) a popular use of the food.

CORN

Every child in public schools in the United States is treated to the story of Squanto teaching the Pilgrims to plant corn with a dead fish in the middle of the hole. The maize of North America became so important throughout the world that it took on the name *corn*, which had been used in earlier times for any grain at all. We probably have a thousand different ways to use corn, including corn on the cob, grits, hominy, popcorn, corn oil, cornstarch, corn meal, and, of course, corn tortillas for tacos. Corn undoubtedly saved the first colonists from starvation and later served the same function in other parts of the world.

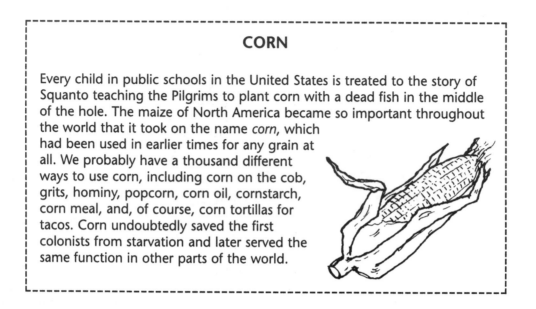

PEANUT

A peanut is, of course, not a nut but rather a legume which grows under the ground. Portuguese explorers found the peanut in South America and took it home and then to Africa, where it was cultivated extensively. Peanuts were then put on slave ships as a food that could be stored for the long voyage. Peanuts, like sweet potatoes, were regarded as food fit for slaves who were allowed to grow them. It was not until the Civil War that peanut oil was used extensively or that a taste for the peanut was developed among whites. It took two people to get this American staple

going, a doctor in St. Louis, who invented peanut butter and promoted it at the World's Fair as a health food, and George Washington Carver, who touted its many uses and promoted its being grown in the worn-out soil of the southeast.

CHOCOLATE

The conquistadors found the Aztec emperor, Montezuma, drinking a beverage made from the beans of the cacao tree. It did not contain sugar, but rather a significant amount of hot peppers. Even today, Mexicans make a chocolate-based molé sauce for meat that is not sweet. The Spaniards became fond of the chocolate drink once sugar replaced the peppers, and they took it back to Spain. A Dutchman developed a method of pressing the oil from the bean, producing both cocoa butter and cocoa powder. In 1847, an English company began making chocolate that could be eaten, which led to the development of milk chocolate in Switzerland and the birth of an addiction.

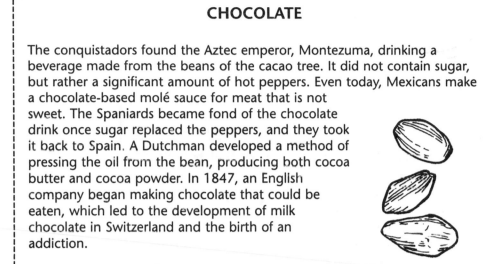

SUGAR

The one food crop that has had perhaps the greatest impact on the Americas did not originate here. Sugar cane is native to Polynesia and moved from there to China and India. It was Columbus who brought sugar to the Caribbean, for by the 1400s it was beginning to supplant honey as the European sweetener. The Spanish began the practice of using slaves to cultivate the cane and thus began the Africanization of the Caribbean. Very soon, English trade goods such as salt, iron bars, cloth, and guns were shipped to West Africa where they were used in bartering with the slave traders. The slaves were sent to the Caribbean, where they were sold to work in the sugar industry. The same ships that brought the slaves were then loaded with raw sugar, molasses, and other sugar products for the return voyage to England. People's taste buds had become dependent on sugar, which in turn was dependent on slavery.

THE SWEET POTATO

The sweet potatoes that Columbus encountered in the West Indies, called *batata*, were light, almost sweet, very starchy, and related to the morning glory family. Slaves confused them with the yams of Africa, which are an entirely different plant. Thus, the dark orange sweet potato is often called a yam, while the white Andean cousin inherited the name potato. When the Spaniards and Portuguese began traveling to the Far East, the sweet  potato went along. In Japan, the sweet potato was used in a variety of food dishes from ice cream to noodles and for a most potent alcoholic drink. In North America, the sweet potato was associated with African Americans, because during slavery it was a food crop they were allowed to cultivate.

THE WHITE POTATO

Perhaps the best-known food to move from the new world to the old is the white potato. It was taken to Europe by early explorers, where it was first used for cattle feed, except in Ireland, which had need of a staple food other than fish. It was grown high in the Andes where corn could not be cultivated. It moved from Spain to France, where it was thought at first to be poison and only good as an ornamental plant. By the 1700s, it had progressed to being considered as food for the poor and prisoners, since potatoes required only a fourth to a sixth of the land that it took to grow the same nutritional value in grain.

TOMATO

The tomato was discovered in Mexico by Cortés, who thought the red fruit would cause some interest at home. It was at first considered poisonous and possibly narcotic, since it belonged to the deadly nightshade family. It came back to North America and was cultivated by Thomas Jefferson, who wrote of several different varieties. But it was the Italians who combined a sauce made from the plant with pasta and brought it back to the New World as they immigrated.

Make a Time Line

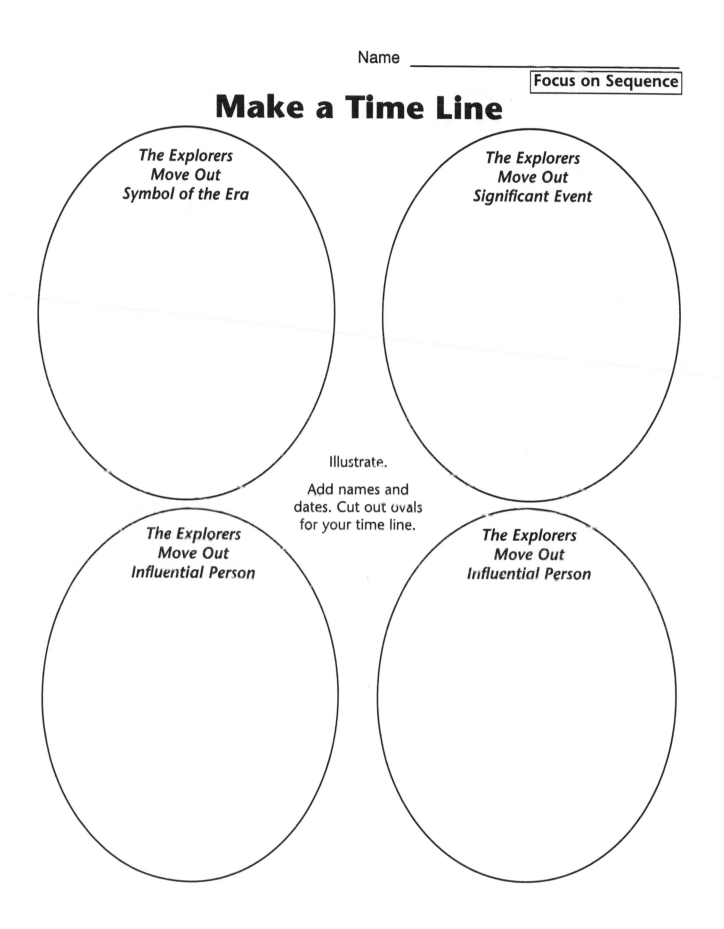

*The Explorers
Move Out
Symbol of the Era*

*The Explorers
Move Out
Significant Event*

Illustrate.

Add names and
dates. Cut out ovals
for your time line.

*The Explorers
Move Out
Influential Person*

*The Explorers
Move Out
Influential Person*

Moving to the New World

The following paragraphs describe the different groups who traveled to the New World and their motivations for doing so.

- The first permanent English colony in North America was built at Jamestown in 1607 on a swampy peninsula. It was not until 1614 that the Virginians found a profitable product that could be sold in Europe. This product, a milder variety of tobacco brought from the West Indies, put the colony on its feet financially.

- Whereas harsh laws made Virginians work together, it was a desire to fulfill God's will that made the Puritans in New England pull together in the 1620s. A bit farther south, the early settlers in New York and New Jersey were the practical Dutch and in Delaware the hard-working Swedes.

- Being a Catholic in England at this time was even worse than being a Puritan. When Lord Baltimore became a Catholic, he was unable to continue his career in the government. At his request, King Charles granted him a charter for 10 million acres of land north of Virginia. The new colony was named Maryland for the queen.

- The first German immigrants arrived in the 1680s from the western part of Germany. They were attracted to Pennsylvania by William Penn, whose successful advertising campaign stressed a policy of complete religious freedom. Hard-working and frugal Lutherans and Mennonites came to escape being forced into European armies. They were not interested in politics, but rather they were dedicated farmers who produced grains, beef, hams, and hides for tanning into leather.

- Slavery existed in all of the colonies, but it became most important in the South, where most slaves remained unskilled, working in rice and tobacco fields. The great majority of slaves had been kidnapped from West Africa. They had been sold to European slave traders and shipped across the Atlantic Ocean under extremely brutal conditions to become the backbone of plantation life.

Many different groups of people moved to the New World, each bringing a particular strength. But no matter the motivation, each group made its own special contribution.

Just for Teachers

Background Information

At this time, western European countries were engaged in a fierce competition for prestige and power. Colonies in the New World could provide the mother countries with valuable materials and help build up trade, thereby providing money to pay for armies and navies. Many new arrivals, however, came for entirely different reasons. Some came because life was intolerable at home; others came purely for adventure. Still others came because they were brought completely against their will. Nevertheless, they brought skills for forging a new nation.

Student pages

Focus on Research **Settlement of the Eastern Seaboard**

On this page, students contrast the different groups of people that began settling in different places along the Eastern Seaboard. By using information found in textbooks and other resources, students answer the questions, providing them a reference for doing the other activities.

Focus on Skills **Contributions to the New Colonies**

Duplicate enough content maps for each pair of students. The content map should be cut apart so it can be put back together in a manner similar to a jigsaw. Cut between the topic "They Came Together" and the names of the groups of people, between the people and the locations, and between the locations and the descriptors. Some sets of descriptors may be cut into two parts. Place each map puzzle into an envelope with the title glued on the outside. Although this is a very simple activity, it will establish a familiarity with cognitive mapping and set the scene for the thinking maps that are required in later sections.

Pairs of students place the parts of the content map together into a prepared envelope. The first class that deals with this activity can actually make the envelopes and then exchange them with one another. The purpose is to make students familiar with the organizational plan provided by semantic mapping. This content map provides a very simple graphic representation of such thinking.

After pairs have put together the content map, ask each student to write a paragraph comparing two of the groups described. Students then explain at least one way the two groups are alike and one way they differ.

Focus on Maps | *They Came to the New World*

This map of the original colonies from 1745 has empty arrows indicating where different groups of people might be going to settle in the New World. Have students label and color the colonies and write the names of the groups and the reasons for coming to the New World inside the arrows.

Focus on Writing | *Design William Penn's Flier*

When William Penn wanted to encourage people to come to his new colonies, he sent recruiters throughout Central Europe carrying pamphlets describing the colony. Penn promised settlers land, low taxes, a representative assembly, and religious freedom for all. Have students design a flier they think might entice new settlers to Pennsylvania.

Hands-On Activity | *Triangular Trade Sandwich*

Students will make peanut butter and molasses open-faced sandwiches as a symbolic representation of the triangular trade (New England to Africa with rum, back to the West Indies with slaves, and then return to Boston with molasses to make more rum). This is similar in intent to the graphic representations of meaningful relationships between concepts provided in cognitive mapping. Thus, a geometric shape is combined with familiar foods to create a symbolic representation of a historical concept which had great impact for a large segment of our population. Prepare enough small plastic bags for every pair of students in the class. In each bag place two slices of bread, a plastic knife and spoon, a stick of candy, two napkins, a few pieces of candy or a roll of Smarties, and two empty medicine cups. Bring a jar of peanut butter and a bottle of molasses to fill the medicine cups. After making the sandwiches, each student will be responsible for filling out the activity sheet.

Focus on Sequence | *Make a Time Line*

This section ends with a time line page. Directions for making a fan-fold time line booklet are given in "The Explorers Move Out" section.

Name _____

Settlement of the Eastern Seaboard

The groups of people who settled in North America during the colonial period came for a variety of different reasons, bringing a variety of different skills. Make notes here about the different groups and the influences upon them.

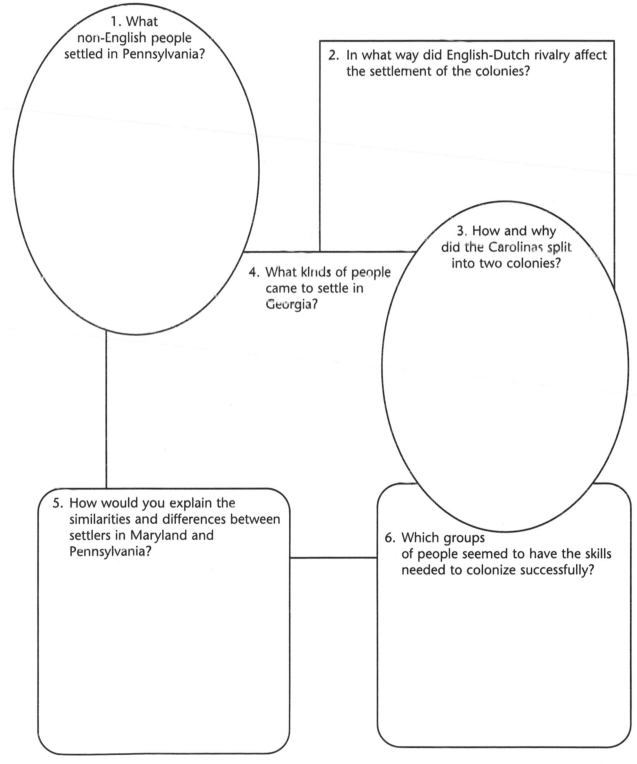

1. What non-English people settled in Pennsylvania?

2. In what way did English-Dutch rivalry affect the settlement of the colonies?

3. How and why did the Carolinas split into two colonies?

4. What kinds of people came to settle in Georgia?

5. How would you explain the similarities and differences between settlers in Maryland and Pennsylvania?

6. Which groups of people seemed to have the skills needed to colonize successfully?

Contributions to the New Colonies

The content map below is to be cut apart so it can be put back together like a jigsaw. Cut between the topic, the groups of people, the locations, and the descriptors. Place the pieces of the content map puzzle into an envelope with the title glued on the outside.

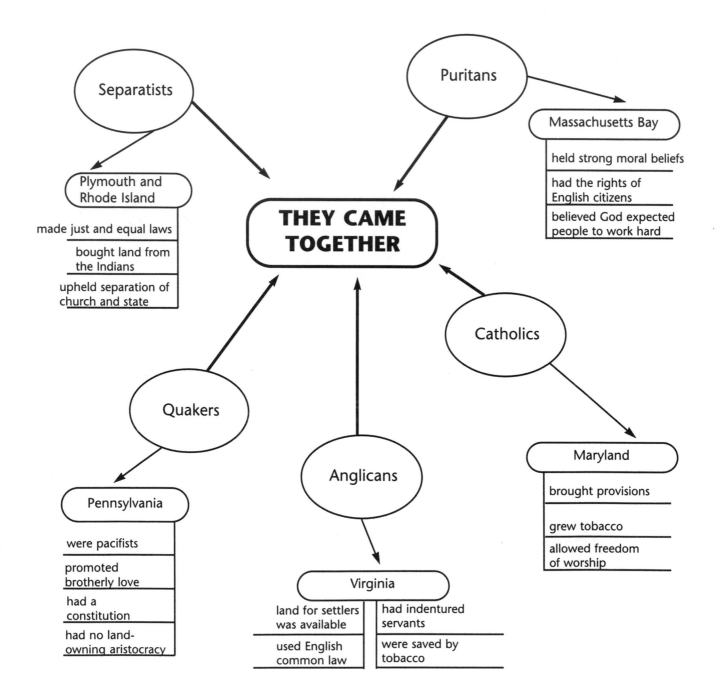

Separatists

Puritans

Massachusetts Bay

held strong moral beliefs

had the rights of English citizens

believed God expected people to work hard

Plymouth and Rhode Island

made just and equal laws

bought land from the Indians

upheld separation of church and state

THEY CAME TOGETHER

Catholics

Quakers

Anglicans

Maryland

brought provisions

grew tobacco

allowed freedom of worship

Pennsylvania

were pacifists

promoted brotherly love

had a constitution

had no land-owning aristocracy

Virginia

land for settlers was available

had indentured servants

used English common law

were saved by tobacco

They Came to the New World

Label and color the original colonies on the map below. In the arrows, write the names of the groups of people who were settling there and their reason(s) for coming to the New World.

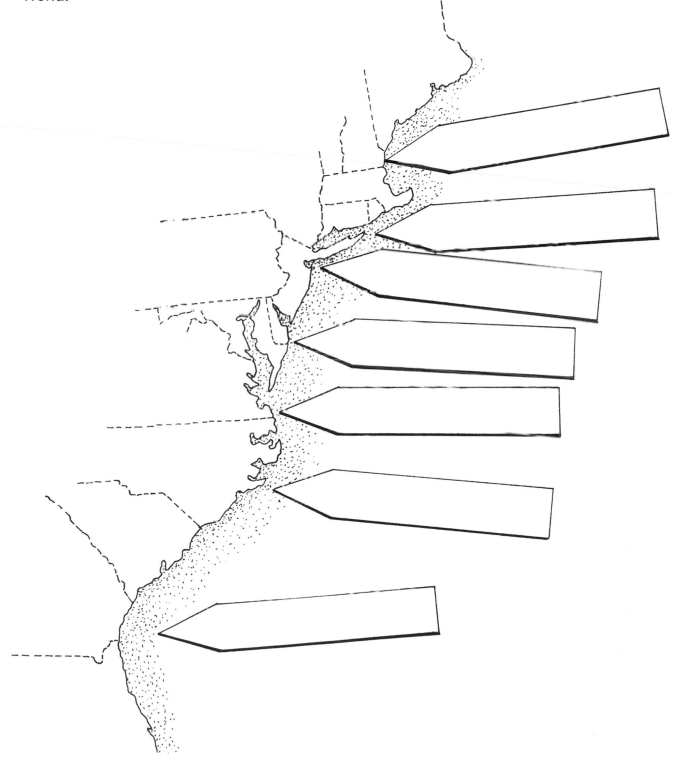

Design William Penn's Flier

When William Penn wanted to encourage people to come to his new colonies, he sent advertisements throughout Central Europe. His agents were emphasizing land, low taxes, a representative assembly, and religious freedom for all. Design a flier you think might entice new settlers to Pennsylvania.

A Brief Description
of
The Provinces
of
CAROLINA
On the Coasts of Florida
and
More particularly of a New-Plantation
begun by the ENGLISH at Cape-Feare
the 29th of May, 1664

The Healthfulness of the Air, The
Fertility of the Earth and Water's
and the great pleasure and profit
will accure to those that shall go.

This is how pamphlets for other colonies tended to look.

Nova Britania
OFFERING MOST

Excellent fruits by planting in

VIRGINIA
It will be exciting for all who see it!

London
1609

Triangular Trade Sandwich

Things with three parts are often labeled *triangular*. So it is with the triangular trade, because the ship captains had three basic ports of call. First, make this open-faced sandwich, and then fill in the blanks to explain the elements of triangular trade that it represents.

Take a slice of bread and, using a plastic knife, cut out a large triangle. Spread the triangle with peanut butter. Outline the triangle with three sticks of candy to emphasize that the triangular trade was dependent on the slavery of the African American. Cover the peanut butter with a thin layer of molasses instead of jelly to emphasize what the slaves were producing. Mark each of the destinations with the candy and toppings provided.

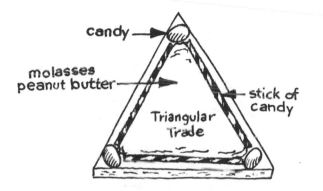

1. The triangle represents _____.

2. The _____ represents the fact that the trade was dependent on black slaves from Africa.

3. Molasses is made from _____ _____. When molasses is distilled it becomes _____.

4. The peanut represents the staples of a slave's diet, which white people did not eat. The type of food on today's menu that came down from early African-American cooking is called _____ _____.

5. I put a _____ on one corner to represent _____. On the second corner I put a _____ to represent _____. And on the third corner, I put a colored candy _____ to represent _____.

Once you have finished the activity, you may eat the triangle.

Make a Time Line

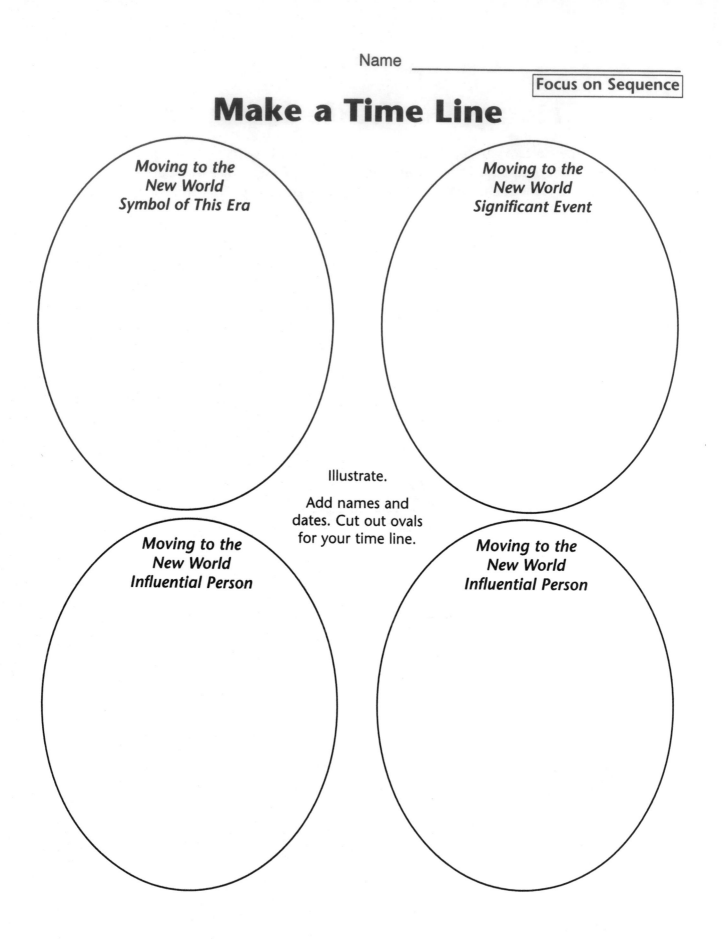

*Moving to the
New World
Symbol of This Era*

*Moving to the
New World
Significant Event*

Illustrate.

Add names and
dates. Cut out ovals
for your time line.

*Moving to the
New World
Influential Person*

*Moving to the
New World
Influential Person*

Moving Toward Independence

The war with France in which Great Britain won vast new lands in North America also created huge debts. At the same time, the colonists, who no longer had to fear the French, were feeling far more independent. Because most male colonists possessed property and the right to vote, they became involved in the world of political debate.

When the British attempted to raise money in 1765 by requiring a tax stamp on all public documents, newspapers, notes and bonds, and other printed paper, it was too much. Although this act was repealed, it was followed by many others just as intolerable. The colonials declared that they possessed the same rights and liberties as did the British at home, but they were not being heard in Great Britain. The colonists also feared the British army of about 6,000 men, thinking that the soldiers might be employed not against the Indians, but against the colonials themselves, should they prove difficult to govern. Their fears would be realized sooner than they knew.

Angry colonists wrote letters to the newspapers and the news traveled from colony to colony. Men and women joined the Sons of Liberty or the Daughters of Liberty so they could make their protests heard. From this fury, great leaders emerged in all of the colonies. Sam Adams and his cousin John in Massachusetts fought in the courts, and Patrick Henry and Thomas Jefferson in Virginia were heard in the House of Burgesses. Finally, after the Boston Massacre, delegates from all of the colonies except Georgia gathered in Philadelphia in 1776 to write the Declaration of Independence. These leaders met again for the First Continental Congress in October of 1777 and had a second chance to exchange ideas with their fellow patriots. But before they could meet again the following year, fighting had already begun in Massachusetts.

Just for Teachers

Background Information

As the British tried to get the colonists to help pay for running the empire, they only succeeded in causing antagonism and violence. By the time there was bloodshed at Lexington and Concord in 1775, all hope of compromise was over. American patriots declared their freedom and went to war. It was not until the Treaty of Paris in 1783, however, that the world formally recognized that colonial ties with Great Britain had been broken and a new nation formed.

Comprehension of current events and wisdom in planning for the future depend upon an understanding of the events of the past and how they have influenced the present. Appreciation of the achievements of those people who helped shape our nation is part of that understanding.

Finding a way of making a mental or thinking map of this information helps place such important ideas in larger contexts. A cognitive or content map refers to an organizing of the textual information in some kind of graphic manner. Students often find this way of summarizing material much more useful than the traditional outline.

Student pages

| Focus on Skills | *Political, Economic, and Social Causes of the American Revolution* |

Each group of three students needs a poster board and three different colored large markers. Students will consider life in the American colonies in the 1600s and early 1700s and then create a cognitive map on a sheet of poster board. In this mental map they will show the political, economic, and social conditions leading to the American Revolution.

Before making the assignment, students might well be shown the Octopus Content Map of Colonial Life so they can apply the methodology in organizing information for their own posters. Explain to students that they will be creating posters in the same manner. The topic will be different, but the technique will be the same. First, they have to decide as a group what they want the poster to look like. Then they are to assign one category to each member of the group. That person will find those events that fall within the chosen category and write them on the chart in the same color. A fourth color is available for outlining and writing the topic.

Have each group show its content map and explain the manner in which the information will be portrayed.

Focus on Maps   *From Colonies to States*

Have students label each of the original 13 colonies on the map. They should then list the names of as many famous leaders from each area as they can, using their textbooks as a resource.

Focus on Writing   *Writing a Bio-Historical Poem*

Separate students into groups and give each group one of the biographical sketches of the Founders of Our Nation. Students are to read the biographical information, or you may want one person to read the information aloud to the group. In order to agree on some of the items in the longer bio-poem, students may have to make inferences. When the reading is finished, the group is responsible for writing a bio-historical poem about the person. When the poems have been completed, they can be cut out and placed on the bulletin board. You may want to have a group responsible for more than one person. Each group should read its bio-poem to the class so that all students are aware of each of the famous people. The completed poems make a wonderful student-constructed bulletin board.

Focus on Sequence   *Make a Time Line*

This section ends with a time line page. Directions for making a fan-fold time line booklet are given in "The Explorers Move Out" section.

Political, Economic, and Social Causes of the American Revolution

The following Octopus Content Map of Colonial Life is one way of showing the way the content of a particular topic might be organized. You will be creating a poster of the causes of the American Revolution. Consider life in the American colonies in the 1600s and early 1700s and then create a content map of the political, economic, and social conditions leading to the American Revolution.

First, you should decide as a group what you want the poster to look like and sketch the basic design on a sheet of poster board. Then each group member takes one category, finds those events that apply, and writes them on the chart in the same color. Be ready to show your content map and explain the manner in which you decided to portray the information.

Octopus Content Map of Aspects of Colonial Life

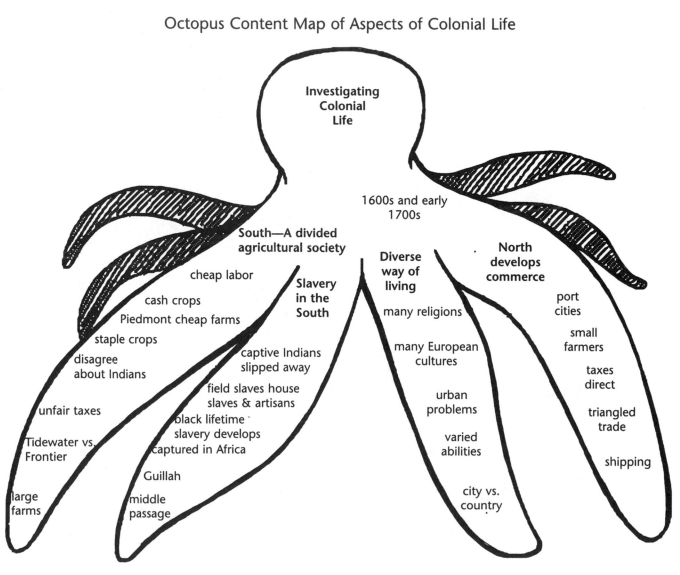

From Colonies to States

Label each of the original 13
colonies on this map. Write in the
names of as many famous leaders
from each of these colonies as you
can find in your textbook.

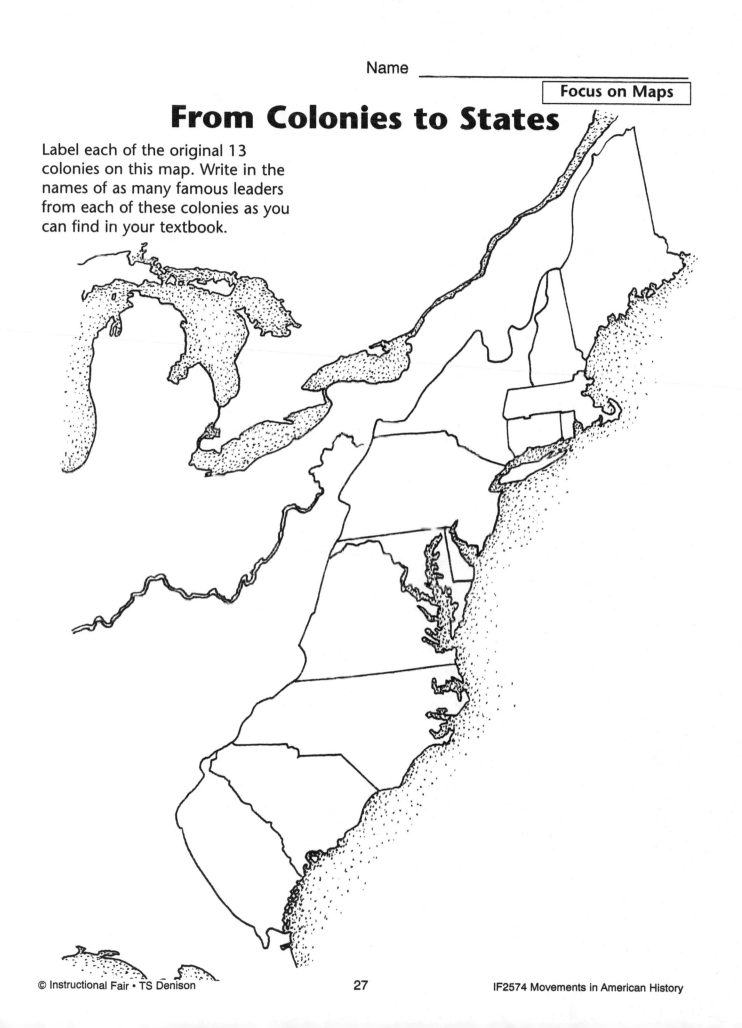

Founders of Our Nation

Lafayette

The Marquis de Lafayette was a French nobleman whose military skills made him an American hero. He helped the colonists during the Revolutionary War against Great Britain by showing them how to train. Named Marie Joseph Paul Yves Roch Gilbert du Motier, he inherited the title Marquis de Lafayette when his grandfather died.

Even as a boy, Lafayette was studying to be a soldier. In 1777, when he was 19, he became excited by the American colonies' fight for independence and decided to go to America and help fight against Great Britain, which was an enemy of France. The Americans welcomed such a well-trained young soldier, making him a major general and sending him into battle immediately. He became a friend of the colonies' commander, George Washington. For four years, Lafayette helped the colonial troops until 1781, when he commanded one of the armies that surrounded the British and made them surrender. Lafayette returned home to France to become a leader in the French Revolution.

Crispus Attucks

Crispus Attucks was an American revolutionary patriot who was killed in the Boston Massacre. It is thought that Attucks was born a slave in approximately 1723 in Massachusetts and that he escaped and worked on sailing ships. He was in Boston at a time when many colonists were angered by the presence of British troops.

People were attacking soldiers on the streets of Boston. On the evening of March 5, 1770, as the bells tolled calling more people into the streets, a crowd of Boston men, including Attucks, confronted a small party of British soldiers and pelted them with sticks and snowballs packed around stones. Someone shouted, "Fire!" and the soldiers fired into the crowd. Samuel Gray, a rope maker, James Caldwell, a sailor, and a very tall black man named Crispus Attucks were killed immediately and two others died soon after from their wounds. Angry colonists called this the Boston Massacre. A memorial to the five men stands today on Boston Common.

John Paul Jones

Known today as the "Father of the United States Navy," John Paul Jones was a naval hero of the Revolutionary War. His real name was simply John Paul. He was born in Scotland in 1747 and went to sea at the age of 12. On board ship, the small, thin Scotsman quickly learned how to sail and soon was able to navigate. By age 21, John Paul had become a sea captain. The young captain was very strict with his crew. He harshly punished those who did not follow his orders. This led some of his crew to mutiny. A crewman was killed, and Paul was accused of murder. He escaped to America to avoid trial and took the last name of Jones to disguise himself.

John Paul Jones joined the new American Navy at the beginning of the Revolutionary War. He served on the first ship to fly the new nation's flag. The Continental Congress gave Jones command of a new ship, the *Ranger*, in which he sailed to Great Britain to raid British ports and ships.

By 1779, Jones was placed in charge of an old, slow ship, the *Bonhomme Richard*, with which he attacked a British ship much larger than his own. Seeing Jones' ship near sinking, the British captain shouted, "Are you ready to surrender?" Jones is said to have replied, "Sir, I have not yet begun to fight!" His ship did sink, but the Americans went on to win the battle.

Congress honored John Paul Jones with a gold medal. Since the United States no longer had need of a navy or the brave captain, he then served in the Russian Navy. After his death in 1792, he was buried at the U.S. Naval Academy.

Thomas Paine

Thomas Paine was born in Great Britain and came to the American colonies in 1774. In January 1776, Thomas Paine published an important pamphlet, *Common Sense*, which urged the colonists to declare their independence from Great Britain.

In his pamphlet, Paine argued that the war ended all hope that Great Britain and the colonies could resolve their differences. In any case, no settlement between the colonies and Great Britain could last. The colonists should declare their independence and get other European countries to help them in the war with Great Britain.

Paine argued against a governmental structure with a king and House of Lords with members who inherited their titles. He claimed that hereditary rule was wrong and dangerous. Paine's pamphlet was read widely from New England to Georgia. It was soon published in Britain, the Netherlands, and France as well.

Patrick Henry

Patrick Henry is best known for being the speaker of those fiery words, "Give me liberty or give me death," as he urged Virginians to fight against British rule. This famous American patriot was governor of Virginia during the Revolutionary War.

Born in Virginia in 1736, his talent for public speaking made him a successful lawyer. Henry was elected to Virginia's House of Burgesses in 1765, the same year that the British government passed the Stamp Act, which placed a tax on all colonial newspapers, calendars, pamphlets, and legal papers. Henry spoke in the House against the Stamp Act and against the British king, George III. Those loyal to the king called his words treason against Britain. "If this be treason, make the most of it," was his well-known reply.

At first, Patrick Henry was opposed to the Constitution when it was drawn up. He thought a strong central government might not do enough to protect the rights of individuals. With his help, the Bill of Rights was added to the Constitution. Henry served five terms as Virginia's governor. He later won a seat in the Virginia state legislature, but died right after the election in 1799.

Samuel Adams

The Adams family of Massachusetts is one of the most remarkable families in American history. The first of the Adams family to make his mark in American history was Samuel, an older cousin of John Adams, our second president. Born in 1722, Samuel Adams became a political leader in Massachusetts. When the colony was arguing with Great Britain over taxes, Sam Adams wrote newspaper articles urging the colonists to stand up for their rights. In 1773, he helped organize the Boston Tea Party to protest a British tax on tea.

Later, Sam Adams represented his state in the two Continental Congresses. At these meetings, the problems with Britain were discussed by men from all the colonies. Adams was one of the first to favor war against Great Britain. Partly because of Samuel Adams' arguments, the Second Continental Congress declared independence from Great Britain.

Paul Revere

Paul Revere was an American patriot who warned the people of Lexington, Massachusetts, that British troops were coming. The story is told in Henry Wadsworth Longfellow's poem "Paul Revere's Ride." Revere was one of the patriots who dumped British tea into Boston Harbor in 1773.

Revere was born in Boston, Massachusetts, in 1735. The son of a silversmith, he learned his father's trade and later took over the family business. Pieces of his artistry are displayed in museums across the country.

When revolutionary leaders in Boston learned that British troops were planning to march on Concord, Revere arranged to signal the patriots with lanterns in a Boston church steeple. One lantern would mean the British were moving by land. Two would mean they were coming by sea. Then, on the night of April 18, two lanterns burned in the North Church steeple. Revere rode to Lexington to warn of the British approach. He then galloped toward Concord, warning patriots along the way. Revere was captured by British scouts, but released. Later, he fought in the Revolutionary War.

When the war ended, Revere took up his trade as a silversmith again. By the time he died in 1818, his fame as a craftsman was equal to his fame as a patriot.

Thomas Jefferson

Thomas Jefferson was a great thinker whose ideas helped shape the United States Constitution and the way the government runs. He was the third president of the United States and the author of the Declaration of Independence. But Jefferson was not only a politician. He helped start the University of Virginia, designed the Virginia Capitol and his own home, Monticello, played the violin, and invented a number of useful things.

Jefferson was born in Albemarle County, Virginia, in 1743 to a wealthy landowner who made certain his son studied history, literature, Greek, Latin, French, Spanish, and Italian. At age 16, he went to Virginia's College of William and Mary to study mathematics, science, and law and became a lawyer at age 24. Jefferson was a governor of Virginia and then became minister to France. He became president of the United States in 1801. During his presidency, he persuaded Congress to agree to the Louisiana Purchase. He died on July 4, 1826, 50 years to the day after the Declaration of Independence was signed.

Jefferson was elected to the Virginia legislature and represented Virginia at the Second Continental Congress. When the congress decided to declare the colonies free of Great Britain, Jefferson was asked to write a statement explaining why this was a necessity for the American people. He took a little over two weeks to write the Declaration of Independence He approved of the new Constitution but wanted a statement in it that protected individual rights. He was largely responsible for the content of the Bill of Rights.

Anne Hutchinson

Anne Hutchinson was a Puritan in the Massachusetts Bay Colony who claimed that God spoke to his saints directly. The Puritan leaders taught that God spoke to people through the Bible, their ministers, and their public officials. The idea that God spoke to individuals directly seemed to them not only wrong but also dangerous, since such people would obey what they said God told them, not the laws of church and state.

Hutchinson first expressed her ideas before small groups of women. Then men started attending her meetings. For all practical purposes, Hutchinson was acting like a minister. Women were not supposed to lead meetings. For a woman to step out of her place in the social order to act like a man was thought shocking and dangerous.

In November 1637, the General Court banished Anne Hutchinson from the colony. She was allowed to stay only through the winter because she was expecting a child. Hutchinson and her family made their way to Rhode Island the next spring. There she helped found the town of Portsmouth.

John and Abigail Adams

John Adams was a lawyer from Massachusetts who became our second president. He was much more cautious than his second cousin, Samuel, but his knowledge of British law earned him the respect of many colonists. And his persistence as a negotiator helped the country to be recognized as a free and independent nation in the Treaty of Paris, which was signed exactly eight years after the first shot was fired at Lexington. The day after the Boston Tea Party, he wrote in his diary, "The people should never rise without doing something to be remembered, something notable and striking. This destruction of the tea is so bold, so daring, so firm . . . it must have such important and lasting consequences that I can't help considering it a turning point in history."

During the Revolution, John Adams was away from home for long periods. His wife, Abigail Adams, wrote to him often. She kept him informed about their children and their farm, which she kept going. When the Continental Congress was preparing the Declaration of Independence, she wrote her husband, "By the way, in the new code of laws that I suppose you will make, I wish you would remember the ladies and be more generous and favorable to them than your ancestors. Do not put such unlimited power in the hands of husbands. Remember, all men would be tyrants if they could. We . . . will not regard ourselves as bound by any laws in which we have had no voice or representation."

John Adams replied, "Depend upon it, we know better than to repeal our masculine systems. Although they are in full force, you know they are little more than theory . . . in practice, you know, we are the subjects. We have only the title of masters, and rather than give this up, which would subject us completely to the power of the petticoat, I hope General Washington and all our brave heroes would fight."

Friedrich von Steuben

Friedrich von Steuben from Prussia improved discipline in the American army. Steuben once served in the Prussian army, the best-trained in Europe. A lively person, Steuben kept everybody in good spirits. He showed the Americans how to use bayonets. Most soldiers had not fought with bayonets, so they used them to roast meat over the fire. Although Steuben spoke little English, he soon taught Washington's troops how to march. He ordered each soldier to put his left hand on the shoulder of the man in front of him. Then Steuben began in his German accent, "Von, Two, Tree, Four! Fooorrvarrd march! Von, Two, Tree, Four!"

Charles Cornwallis

After George Washington defeated the Hessians at the Battle of Trenton, the British sent General Charles Cornwallis to recapture the city. On the evening of January 2, Cornwallis saw the lights of Washington's campfires and said, "At last we have run down the old fox and we will bag him in the morning." But Cornwallis was fooled, for Washington left his fires burning and marched to attack Princeton and win another victory. Cornwallis also had problems in the Carolinas. As soon as he set up Loyalist militias to control an area, out came rebels from the swamps or mountains. Cornwallis pulled back into South Carolina, but he was constantly harassed. After the victory at Guilford Court House in North Carolina cost another 500 men, Cornwallis led his army to Chesapeake Bay in Virginia, where he set up camp at Yorktown. When he was prevented from receiving help by sea, the strength of the British army was broken and the proud and aristocratic Cornwallis surrendered in an impressive ceremony.

Ethan Allen

In May 1775, some American troops under Benedict Arnold of Connecticut and Ethan Allen of Vermont seized the British Fort Ticonderoga on Lake Champlain in northern New York. Leading the attack was Ethan Allen, a blacksmith famous for his strength and fierce temper. Allen, whose followers came from the nearby Green Mountains of Vermont, knew that the fort had a good supply of gunpowder and about 100 cannons that the Americans badly needed. Allen and The Green Mountain Boys went directly to the rooms where the officers slept and called out to the British commander, "Come out, you old rat!" The commander pulled on his uniform and demanded to know on whose authority Allen acted. "In the name of the Great Jehovah and the Continental Congress!" he replied.

Benedict Arnold

The key American fort on the Hudson, West Point, was almost sold to the British by its commander, Benedict Arnold. The ambitious Arnold thought the Americans did not appreciate him enough. He had also developed expensive tastes and had many debts. In May 1779, he offered his services to the British—for a price. In 1780, he promised to turn over to the British the garrison at West Point. When Major John André, an aide to British general Sir Henry Clinton, was captured, hidden in his stockings were papers verifying Arnold's treason. Hearing that André had been captured, Arnold fled at breakneck speed to the British. The British kept their word and made him a brigadier general in the king's army and paid him handsomely for his services. Although the Americans remained at West Point, Arnold's treason badly shook General Washington.

Benjamin Franklin

In his long life from 1706 to 1790, Benjamin Franklin rose from poverty to become famous throughout the world. Franklin was one of 17 children of a poor Boston soap and candle maker. He left school at 10 to work for his father and then for his brother James, a printer. At 17, he ran away from Boston and made his way to Philadelphia, where he set up a printing shop. He published pamphlets, newspapers, and almanacs.

From an early age, Franklin was curious about how things worked, and he was full of ideas for improving things. In 1740, he invented the Franklin stove, which looked something like an iron fireplace. He invented the bifocal lens so that people could use the same pair of glasses for both reading and seeing at a distance. He experimented with electricity and in 1752 proved that lightning was a form of electricity. Franklin invented the lightning rod to protect buildings against damage from lightning and a long arm to bring down merchandise from high shelves

Franklin had ideas about improving city life. He convinced Philadelphia to pave its streets with cobblestones, helped organize a police force, and set up a fire company. Eager to promote education, he organized the first lending library in America and an academy that later became the University of Pennsylvania.

George Washington

George Washington was born on February 22, 1732, on a plantation in the colony of Virginia. As a boy, he received little formal schooling, but he showed a gift for mathematics and began training as a surveyor. This work was very important, because new lands were being claimed, bought, and sold. By age 16, he was working as a field surveyor in the Shenandoah Valley of northern Virginia. When his half brother died, the care of the family plantation, Mount Vernon, was left to young George.

Washington joined the Virginia militia and fought in the French and Indian War. His troops were defeated in battle in the Ohio River Valley, but he emerged as commander in chief of the Virginia militia. In 1758, Washington resigned from the militia and returned to Mount Vernon and married a widow named Martha Custis. He also was elected to Virginia's law-making body, the House of Burgesses.

Washington returned to Philadelphia to attend the Second Continental Congress. The Congress voted to send Washington to Boston to take command of the colonial forces. He became the leader of an army of untrained and poorly equipped patriots. He suffered with his troops through cold winters and defeats in battle. After eight years of military service, Washington went home to Mount Vernon. Later he went as Virginia's representative to the Constitutional Convention where he was elected president of the convention. His role during the convention and his fame as a general made him the natural choice to serve as the country's first president. Washington was a strong leader who united the new nation. He spent his last years managing his large farm and died at Mount Vernon.

Writing a Bio-Historical Poem

Read the biographical information given to your group. One person should read it aloud to the group. Be certain you can agree on the occasion that made him or her famous, what this person did that was important, where and when he or she did it, and what kind of personality you think the person had. You may wish to check your history textbook for more detailed information or to see what the person looked like. Then write a bio-historical poem about your group's famous person.

EXAMPLE

William E. B.
Educated, forceful, caring, impatient
Friend of Booker T. Washington
Lover of freedom, equality, education
Who felt angry, worried, inspired
Who needed the right to vote, political power, financial support
Who gave instruction, inspiration, written words
Who feared segregation, Jim Crow laws, discrimination
Who wanted to see equality, freedom for all, universal education
Resident of Massachusetts
DuBois

BIO-HISTORICAL FORMAT

Line 1: First name only
Line 2: Four traits that describe the person
Line 3: Sibling of .....Son of... friend of ....
Line 4: Lover of.... (3 ideas)
Line 5: Who felt....... (3 items)
Line 6: Who needed.... (3 items)
Line 7: Who gave... (3 items)
Line 8: Who feared... (3 items)
Line 9: Who wanted to see ... (3 items)
Line 10. Resident of .....
Line 11: Last name only .....

Try It:

1. _____
2. _____
3. _____
4. _____
5. _____
6. _____
7. _____
8. _____
9. _____
10. _____
11. _____

Name _____

Make a Time Line

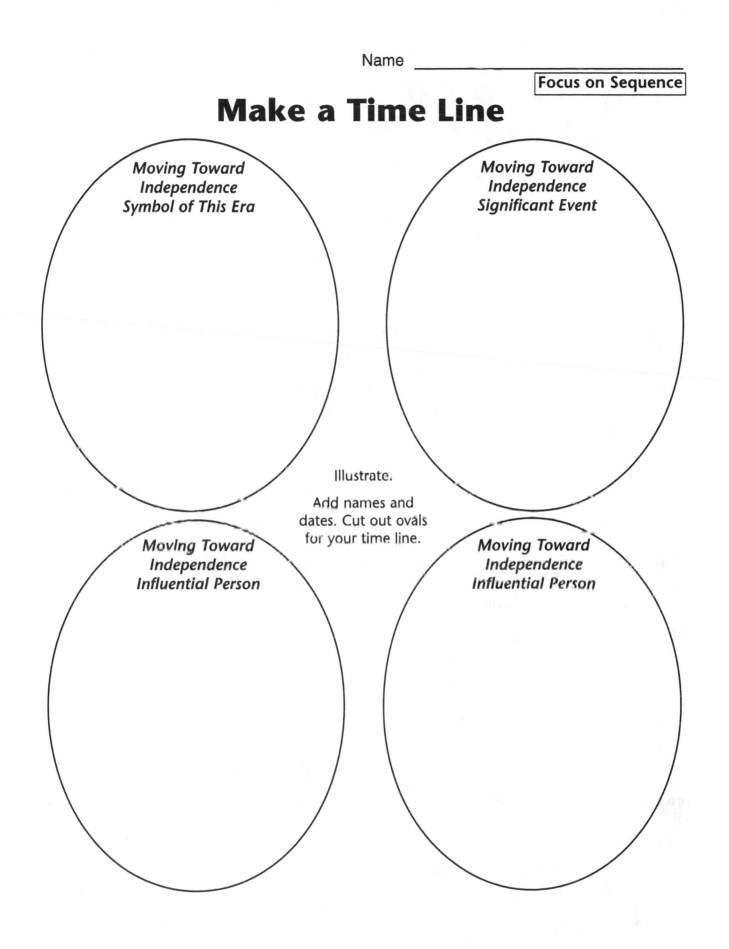

Moving Toward
Independence
Symbol of This Era

Moving Toward
Independence
Significant Event

Illustrate.

Add names and
dates. Cut out ovals
for your time line.

Moving Toward
Independence
Influential Person

Moving Toward
Independence
Influential Person

Moving Toward Democratic Government

Even while the colonists were still struggling for their independence, they began to plan for the kind of government they wanted. The first document agreed upon, The Articles of Confederation, gave almost all of the power to the states. It created a weak national government that could not enforce treaties, raise money, provide courts, regulate trade, or even maintain an army.

Influential Americans demanded that something be done to change the situation. In May of 1787, a group of 55 remarkable men assembled in Philadelphia. Among them were George Washington, James Madison, Benjamin Franklin, Alexander Hamilton, and Robert Morris. Some of the leaders of the Revolution were not present—either because they did not want a strong federal government or because they were representing the United States in Europe.

It soon became clear that it would be necessary to come up with an entirely new plan rather than make a patchwork of changes. The delegates went to work and came up with a document that has been the basis of our government ever since. The bundle of compromises which were hammered out at that time became our best legal invention. It was decided to have a national government of three branches that could check on and balance one another. Terms were set and financial matters arranged. Certain powers were given to the federal government, but others were retained for the states. Provisions were made for changing the document should three fourths of the states approve.

During the process of approving the Constitution, various states asked for amendments that would guarantee that the federal government could not take away the rights of individuals or of states. These guarantees have come to be known as the Bill of Rights.

Just for Teachers

Background Information

All of the new state governments that emerged during and after the Revolutionary War were based on written constitutions. All these new constitutions contained some sort of bill of rights that guaranteed individual freedoms. The attempt to write a national document that guaranteed not only the rights of citizens but also divided powers between states and a federal government was much more complex.

Patrick Henry called this writing of a completely new constitution "a revolution as radical as that which separated us from Great Britain." In fact, the framers fashioned a blueprint for a country that would remain united for well over two centuries. It is a tribute to the wisdom and foresight of its creators.

To understand an interpretation of this constitution, it is important to first understand what was contained in the document itself and the first ten amendments known as the Bill of Rights. The following activities are designed to get students to know something of the content intended by the framers. To help students remember what is in different provisions, you might like to have groups role-play a situation that involves the guarantees. The rest of the class can then guess what is being portrayed.

Student pages

Focus on Research | *Separation of Powers* and *Delegation of Powers*

Have students first look through the Constitution and record information for the large graphic posters they will create as a group. Assign groups to complete posters either about the powers of the three branches of the federal government or about powers guaranteed and denied to the national government and to the individual states. Two ways of organizing the posters are given on the activity sheets, but groups may wish to modify the suggestion to fit the information they have selected to present. When the posters are finished, they should be presented to the class.

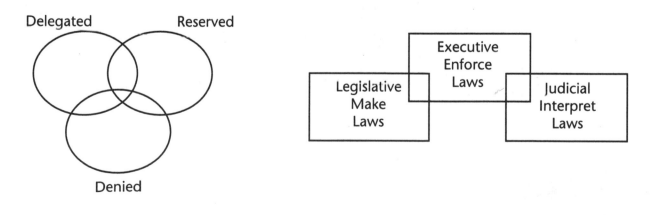

Hands-on Activity | *Matching Up Your Constitutional Rights*

Prepare enough sets of materials to have one for each pair of students. Duplicate sheets and cut each sheet as shown below. Insert each set in an individual envelope and glue the title and directions on the outside.

Students will match the rights guaranteed with the number of the amendment that names that protection.

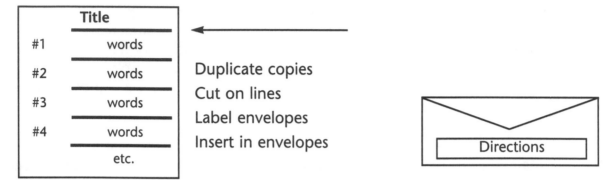

Duplicate copies
Cut on lines
Label envelopes
Insert in envelopes

Directions

Afterwards, have students fold a paper into thirds one direction and then in half the other direction to create nine rectangles when unfolded. In each of the resultant nine parts, students illustrate one right guaranteed by the Constitution and identify the number of the amendment.

Focus on Thinking | *Establishing Amendment Priorities*

The items in this activity, like others in the Democratic Government section, are designed to be cut up, placed in envelopes, and completed by pairs of students. Students place the slip for each amendment in one of two piles, as they decide which to keep and which to discard should the Bill of Rights need to be shortened. Afterwards, groups give reasons for keeping or discarding each amendment.

Focus on Skills | *Categorizing Your Constitutional Rights*

Have students decide in teams how to categorize or group rights guaranteed by the Constitution. First, they must decide on the categories to be used. Afterwards, they decide how each amendment should be classified. Choices are indicated by writing the number of the category beside the amendment.

Focus on Writing *The Purpose of the Bill of Rights*

The items in this activity, like others in the "Moving Toward Democratic Government" section, are designed to be cut up, placed in envelopes, and completed by pairs of students. Students arrange sentences to answer the essay question "What is the purpose of the Bill of Rights and what does it have to say?"

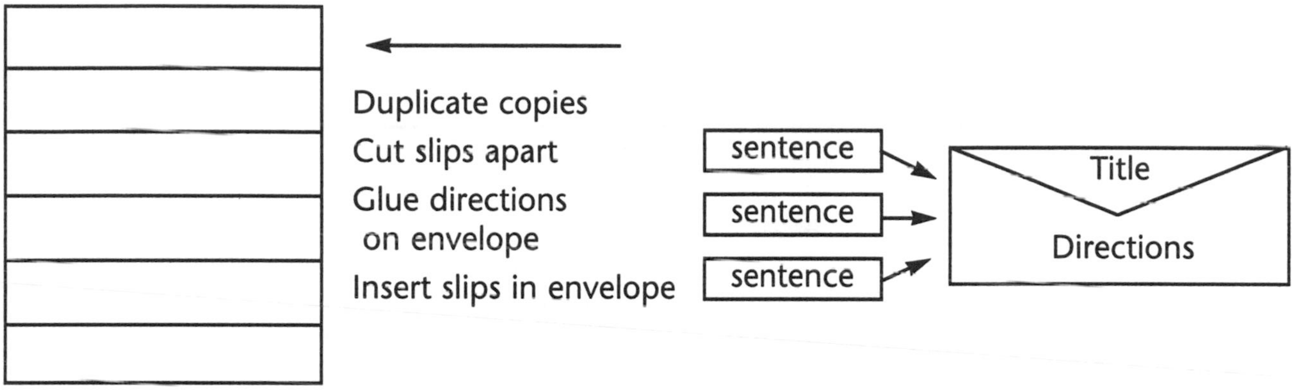

It is useful to use a different color of paper when you start duplicating a new activity. That way, the color of directions on the outside of the envelopes makes them easy to identify. The way the sentences appear on the activity sheet is the most likely order.

Focus on Sequence *Make a Time Line*

This section ends with a time line page. Directions for making a fan-fold time line booklet are given in "The Explorers Move Out" section.

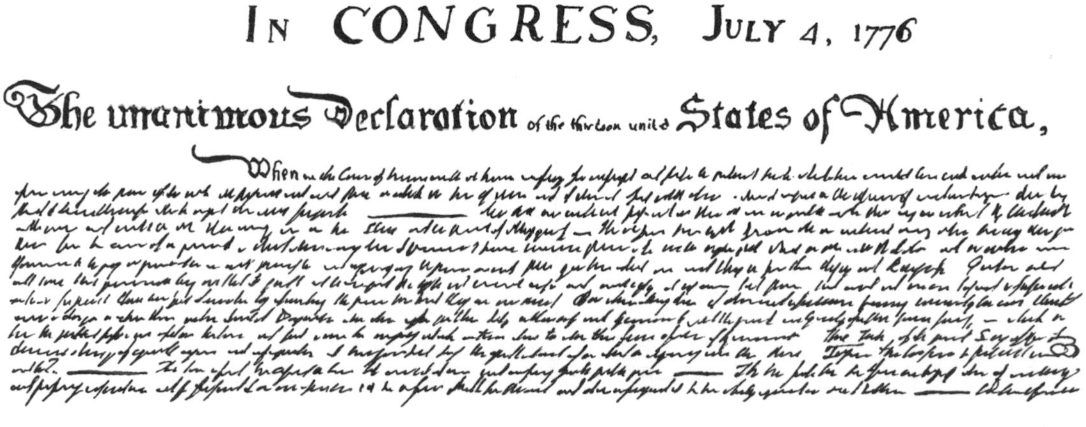
IN CONGRESS, JULY 4, 1776

The unanimous Declaration of the thirteen united States of America,

Separation of Powers

Your task is to create a poster that presents information about the duties and responsibilities of the three branches of the federal government that you find from reading the Constitution. This page can be used to help you plan the organization of your poster.

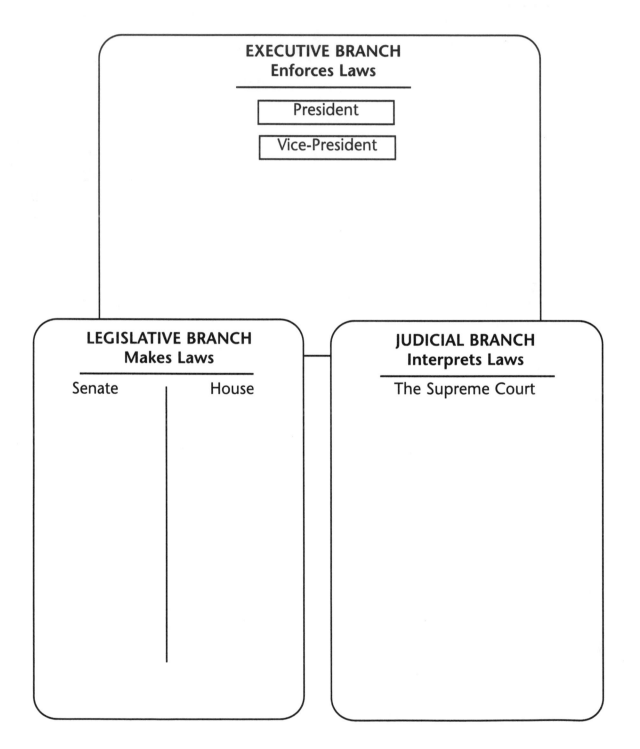

EXECUTIVE BRANCH
Enforces Laws
_____

President

Vice-President

LEGISLATIVE BRANCH
Makes Laws
_____

Senate   House

JUDICIAL BRANCH
Interprets Laws
_____

The Supreme Court

Delegation of Powers

Your task is to create a poster that presents information about the powers given to the federal government, those kept for the states, and those given to both. You will also need to include powers neither one is ever supposed to use. This page can be used to help you plan the organization of your poster.

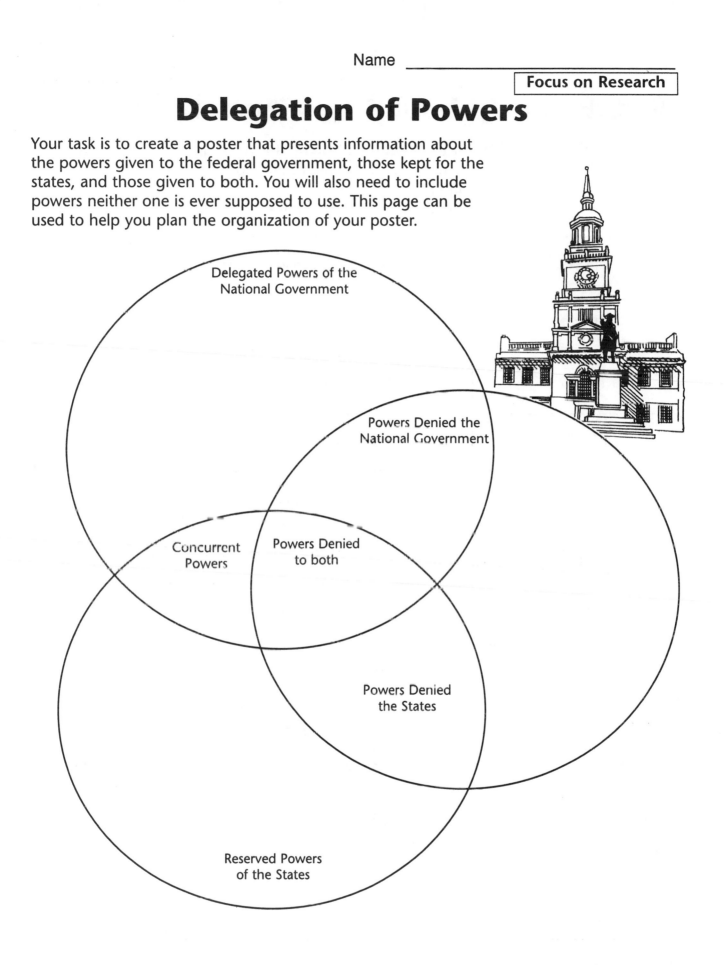

Delegated Powers of the
National Government

Powers Denied the
National Government

Concurrent
Powers

Powers Denied
to both

Powers Denied
the States

Reserved Powers
of the States

Matching Up Your Constitutional Rights

The number of the Amendment to the Constitution has been cut apart from a phrase that tells what is in the amendment. Your task is to match them up. Afterwards, fold a paper into nine parts and in each rectangle illustrate one right guaranteed by the Constitution. Write the number of the amendment in which that right is guaranteed.

FIRST	Freedom of religion, speech, press, assembly
SECOND	Right to bear arms and form a militia
THIRD	No quartering of soldiers in your home
FOURTH	No unreasonable searches and seizures
FIFTH	Right to due process, no self-incrimination
SIXTH	Right to be represented by a lawyer
SEVENTH	Right to jury trial in civil cases
EIGHTH	No unfair punishment, bail, fines
NINTH	Have rights not listed in the constitution
TENTH	Powers not listed belong to states or people

Establishing Amendment Priorities

It has been decided that the Bill of Rights should be shortened. Choose five amendments to keep and five that you might discard. A summary of the rights in each amendment has been placed on a separate slip of paper. Place the slips in two piles—one for keeping and one for discarding. Be prepared to discuss your reasons for keeping or discarding each amendment.

FIRST AMENDMENT

Citizens have the right to freedom of religion, speech, press, getting together in a peaceful group, and to ask the government to correct any injustice.

SECOND AMENDMENT

Citizens have the right to keep and use firearms for national security.

THIRD AMENDMENT

Citizens have the right to refuse soldiers being lodged in their homes.

FOURTH AMENDMENT

Citizens have the right to privacy for themselves, their homes, and their belongings. Any search must be reasonable and must be done according to a search warrant that tells the place and what is being searched for.

FIFTH AMENDMENT

Citizens have rights in court. They cannot be tried twice for the same crime, do not have to testify against themselves, and cannot lose life, liberty, or property without due process of law.

SIXTH AMENDMENT

Citizens in court have the right to a speedy and public trial, a jury in a criminal case, the right to face accusers, and the right to call witnesses.

SEVENTH AMENDMENT

Citizens have a right to a jury trial in a civil case.

EIGHTH AMENDMENT

Citizens have the right to reasonable bail, fines, and punishment.

NINTH AMENDMENT

Citizens have rights not listed in the Constitution.

TENTH AMENDMENT

Powers not listed and given to the federal government belong to states or people.

Categorizing Your Constitutional Rights

Think about the rights that are guaranteed to you as an individual by the Constitution. Then, decide how you could categorize or group these rights. As a team, decide which categories to use and then how they apply. You do not have to use all of the categories suggested. You can add one of your own. Have a reason for your choices. Place the number of the agreed-upon category beside each amendment.

1. Right to do something
2. Rights when accused of something
3. Right to have something
4. Right to be something
5. (Your choice) _____

FIRST	freedom of religion, speech, press, assembly	_____
SECOND	right to bear arms and form a militia	_____
THIRD	no quartering of soldiers in your home	_____
FOURTH	no unreasonable searches and seizures	_____
FIFTH	right to due process, no self-incrimination	_____
SIXTH	right to be represented by a lawyer	_____
SEVENTH	right to jury trial in civil cases	_____
EIGHTH	no unfair punishment, bail, fines	_____
NINTH	have rights not listed in the Constitution	_____
TENTH	powers not listed belong to states or people	_____
THIRTEENTH	no one can be held in slavery	_____
FOURTEENTH	guaranteed due process and equal protection	_____
NINETEENTH	women have the right to vote	_____
TWENTY-SIXTH	can vote from age 18	_____

The Purpose of the Bill of Rights

These sentences should form an answer to this essay question: "What is the purpose of the Bill of Rights and what does it have to say?" Your task is to place the sentences in the correct order. Notice that one of the slips is blank. There is a spot in the paragraph that calls for more specific details. Place the blank slip in that spot and write a sentence that could go there.

The Bill of Rights does not give Americans rights but rather prevents government from taking away certain basic rights that people already have.

The First Amendment guarantees the basic rights of freedom of religion, freedom of speech, freedom of the press, and freedom to meet in groups.

The next three amendments came out of the colonists' struggle with Great Britain.

They deny government the right to quarter soldiers, to conduct unreasonable searches and seizures, and to forbid an arms-bearing militia.

Amendments five through eight protect citizens who are accused of crimes and are brought to trial.

_____
_____
_____.

The last two amendments limit the powers of the federal government to those that are granted in the Constitution.

Because of the rights explained above, citizens of the United States enjoy some very important freedoms.

Name _____

Make a Time Line

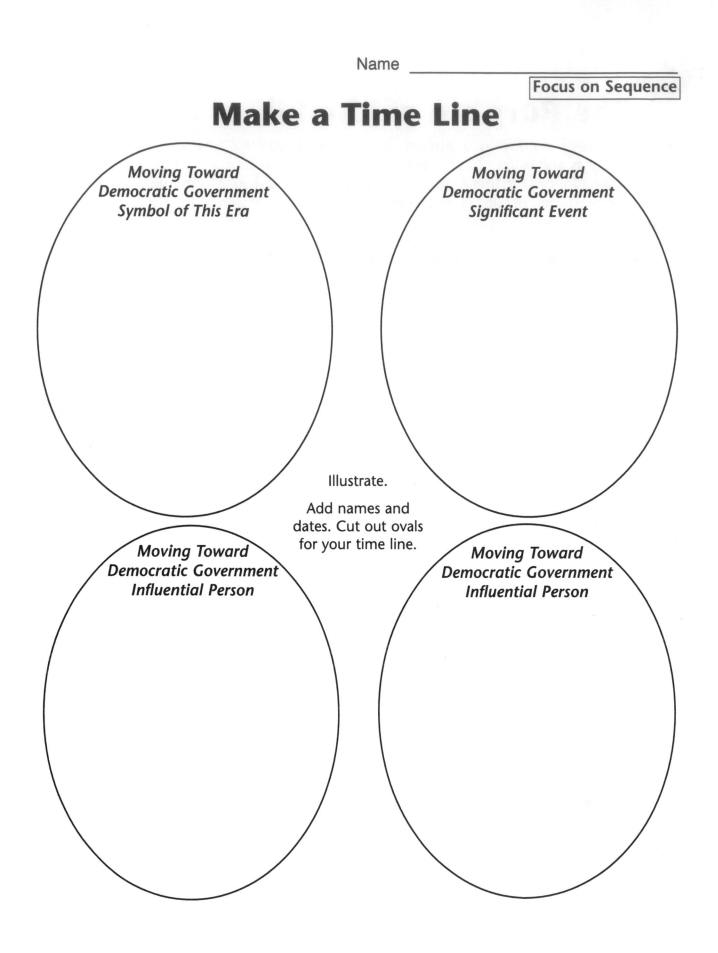

Moving Toward
Democratic Government
Symbol of This Era

Moving Toward
Democratic Government
Significant Event

Illustrate.

Add names and
dates. Cut out ovals
for your time line.

Moving Toward
Democratic Government
Influential Person

Moving Toward
Democratic Government
Influential Person

Moving onto the World Scene

In 1789, George Washington was called to lead a country of less than four million people. Most of those people lived in villages or on farms and plantations. Not many lived in cities, which were very small by today's standards. Factories as we know them hardly existed; most things were made at home or in small workshops. Fifteen years later, the country had doubled in size and Americans had to look beyond their own shores.

The beginning of the nineteenth century was an exciting time in many places throughout the world. In the Americas, 1801 brought the election of Thomas Jefferson to the presidency of the United States. Unfortunately, the British still had not recognized the United States as a sovereign nation. They insisted on boarding ships flying our flag and impressing the sailors into the British Navy. This eventually led to the War of 1812 under President James Madison.

America as a new nation was in jeopardy from several sources. There were Indian wars to the west and impressment at sea. The problems of the national debt had not been settled, and great differences in the interpretation of the Constitution made tempers flare. And, even though the United States had arranged the Louisiana Purchase, European nations still wanted to colonize in certain parts of that territory. Gradually, the new nation was able to negotiate treaties which cleared up its troubled relationship with the rest of the world.

Just for Teachers

Background Information

The troubles that Americans faced in the period between 1801 and 1815 helped draw the country together as a united nation. The Napoleonic Wars had helped Jefferson obtain the Louisiana Territory in 1803, but soon after Madison took office in 1809, the country could not avoid becoming involved in the turmoil. However, the nation emerged from the war without loss of territory, and by 1815, the Indians had been driven out of the Michigan territory and the new state of Ohio. Now the new nation could become economically, politically, and culturally independent from Europe

Using this 15-year period as a backdrop, the activity sheets in this section center on students discovering some of the different ways they learn. These different learning modalities can be highlighted in the following ways:

1. Ask the names of the first five presidents—Washington, Adams, Jefferson, Madison, and Monroe. To know these, we have to **memorize**.
2. Show a map of the United States during the War of 1812. Note the states admitted. Notice the trouble spots. This is **interpreting graphics**.
3. From 1800 until 1815, America's survival was in jeopardy. Some facts that might back up this statement are impressment, Indian Wars, European colonization, Embargo Act, treaties, pirates, and the national debt. This is **using data to back up an opinion**. This data can be recorded on the semantic map provided.
4. Jefferson is a more well-known president than Madison. In fact, Madison's wife Dolley is probably better known than he is. Both men were aristocrats from Virginia, and both were writers. But Madison was a man of ideas who lacked a great leader's power to dominate. If students remember all of this after you mention it, they will be doing **auditory processing,** because they had to listen and relate what was said to what they already knew.
5. Sometimes we have to do some specific kinds of **critical thinking**. The skills activity sheet uses the ability to identify **cause and effect** relationships during these years, followed by a writing activity using cause and effect. As the slips of paper in the envelopes are moved and matched, it is **tactile involvement**.
6. The hands-on activity uses **sequential thinking** to cut and paste a time line of the Jefferson and Madison presidencies. Students may have to use **visual acuity** and look up some information in the book. The cutting and pasting is another form of using the **tactile** or **kinesthetic modality**. Chronological sequencing is also emphasized in the writing activity.

You may want to use a marker to write some of these learning modalities on cards. The cards can be handed to students to show or place on the chalk rail as you finish talking about that specific skill. This will give them a vocabulary for metacognition.

| Focus on Research | *America in Jeopardy Cognitive Map* |

On this cognitive map, students outline several of the factors that placed the United States in jeopardy as the nation began relations with the rest of the world. Information about this topic may be found in almost any American history textbook.

| Focus on Maps | *Trouble Spots* |

Using the map of the United States during the War of 1812, students color the trouble spots in red and then write the name of the place or conflict in the box.

| Focus on Chronology | *From Jefferson to Monroe* |

The emphasis in this activity and the next is developing the related critical thinking skills of chronological sequencing and cause and effect. It is intended for this to enhance the ability to write answers to essay questions. This activity requires preparing envelopes as explained in the "Matching Your Constitutional Rights" activity in the "Moving Toward Democratic Government" section. The envelopes are to be passed out to pairs of students for matching cause and effect.

| Focus on Skills | *The Embargo Act* |

This activity requires students to organize sentences into a logical answer to a typical essay question. Note that the last sentence Is one which does not belong—it is true but irrelevant. The other sentences are in logical order as printed. Cut the sentences apart and place them in envelopes as explained in "The Purpose of the Bill of Rights" activity In the "Moving Toward Democratic Government" section. Practicing these skills should lead students into the paragraph writing requested in the next activity.

| Focus on Writing | *The Panic of 1837* |

Have students match the cause-and-effect statements that tell what led up to the panic of 1837. Afterwards, they combine the ideas to write a well-organized answer to an essay question by using transition words and phrases, such as *however, nevertheless, this caused, subsequently, after that,* and *over time.*

| Hands-On Activity | *A Time Line for Mr. Jefferson* |

After students have gathered the information, each will cut and paste the events on the attached sheet in order to make a time line. The years covered are from 1801, when Jefferson takes office, to 1815, when Madison signed the treaty with Tripoli.

| Focus on Sequence | *Make a Time Line* |

This section ends with a time line page. Directions for making a fan-fold time line booklet are given in "The Explorers Move Out" section.

America in Jeopardy Cognitive Map

In each of the parts of the cognitive map, write one statement of fact that validates the notion that before 1815, America might have been in jeopardy for this reason.

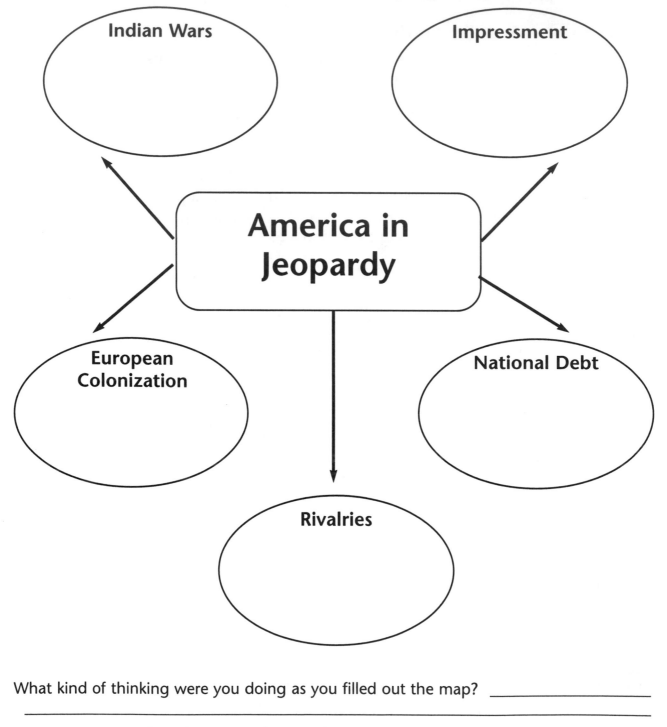

What kind of thinking were you doing as you filled out the map? _____
_____

How can you use the information that you have collected and organized? _____
_____

Trouble Spots

Using this map of the United States during the War of 1812, color the trouble spots in red and then write the names of the places or conflicts in the boxes.

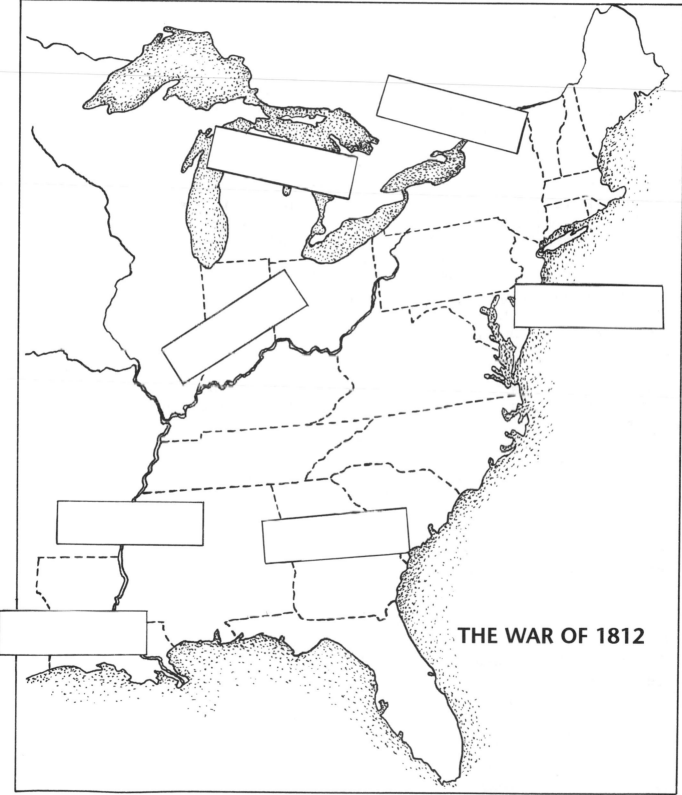

THE WAR OF 1812

From Jefferson to Monroe

Match cause and effect to make sentences about the first part of the nineteenth century.

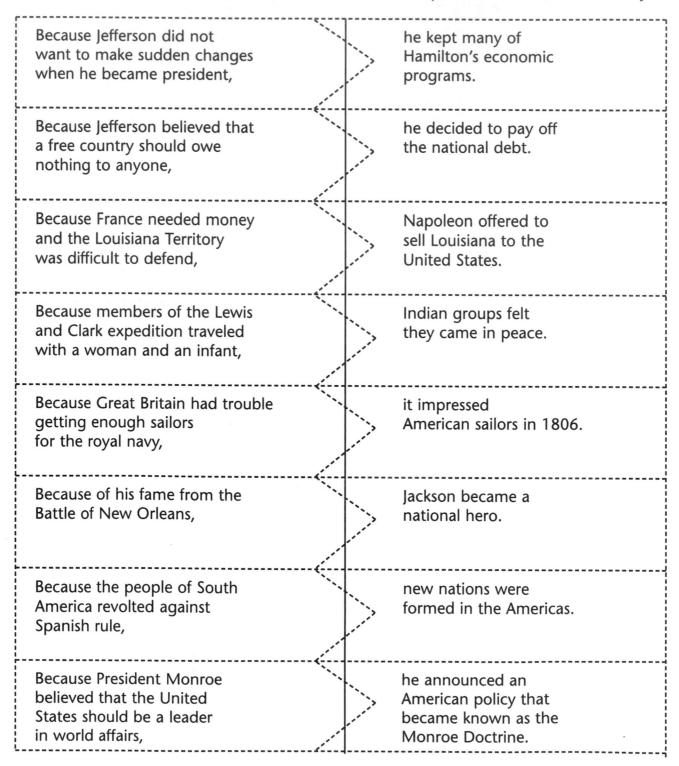

Because Jefferson did not want to make sudden changes when he became president,	he kept many of Hamilton's economic programs.
Because Jefferson believed that a free country should owe nothing to anyone,	he decided to pay off the national debt.
Because France needed money and the Louisiana Territory was difficult to defend,	Napoleon offered to sell Louisiana to the United States.
Because members of the Lewis and Clark expedition traveled with a woman and an infant,	Indian groups felt they came in peace.
Because Great Britain had trouble getting enough sailors for the royal navy,	it impressed American sailors in 1806.
Because of his fame from the Battle of New Orleans,	Jackson became a national hero.
Because the people of South America revolted against Spanish rule,	new nations were formed in the Americas.
Because President Monroe believed that the United States should be a leader in world affairs,	he announced an American policy that became known as the Monroe Doctrine.

The Embargo Act

You have been asked to answer the following essay question:

It is said that Americans suffered more under the Embargo Act than did Britain or France. Explain why you think this statement is either true or false.

The sentences inside this envelope are one person's answer to the question. Place them in order and omit ideas that, while true, do not relate to the question asked. You should expect to put the main idea in the first sentence or two, continue with specific details, and then finish with a general conclusion.

Hoping to avoid war but to hurt France and Great Britain, Jefferson got Congress to pass the Embargo Act in 1807.

Under this act, which forbade the exporting or importing of any goods, Americans suffered the most.

Sailors lost their jobs, and farmers had their wheat and cotton piled high at the docks.

Ordinary citizens could not get anything that was imported, including sugar, salt, tea, and molasses.

This interference with shipping caused general economic hardship, because the American economy was based on exporting agricultural products and importing manufactured goods.

Americans were furious at the British for impressing their sailors and attacking their ships.

The Panic of 1837

Match the cause-and-effect statements that explain this chronology by placing the correct letter in the blank.

___ 1. Because the price of cotton fell . . .

A. they could not repay their bank loans.

___ 2. Because cotton planters had no income . . .

B. cotton planters had no income.

___ 3. Because cotton planters could not repay their bank loans

C. many more banks failed, making their paper worthless.

___ 4. Because some banks were failing . . .

D. banks didn't have enough gold and silver to repay depositors.

___ 5. Because President Jackson had ordered buyers of land to pay with silver or gold . . .

E. depositors demanded their money from all the banks.

___ 6. Because banks did not have enough gold and silver . . .

F. many businesses failed and the depression continued.

___ 7. Because of lack of gold and silver and nonpayment of outstanding loans . . .

G. state banks printed paper money that was not backed by gold or silver.

___ 8. Because people could not cash in their worthless paper money . . .

H. many banks failed because they needed the loan payments for income.

Now write a short paragraph that would answer this essay question: "What caused the Panic of 1837?" You might combine the first ideas in a statement such as: "When the price of cotton fell, the planters had no income and could not repay the loans they had taken out in order to pay for western lands." Try to use transition words and phrases like those in the box.

however	nevertheless	this caused
subsequently	after that	over time

Name _____

A Time Line for Mr. Jefferson

Find some of these events in your textbook and write down the dates on which they happened. Cut apart these boxes and place them on a time line of the years that Thomas Jefferson and James Madison held the office of president.

On March 4, 1801, Thomas Jefferson walked the streets of half-finished Washington, D.C., as the newly elected president. He knew his first job would be to choose a Cabinet that shared his views.	Because the Embargo Act was hurting New England merchants and they protested strongly, Congress replaced it with the Nonintercourse Act, which allowed Americans to trade with all nations except Great Britain and France.
In February, the Supreme Court heard the case of *Marbury* v. *Madison*. Chief Justice Marshall wrote the Court's decision in which judicial review was established.	The United States frigate *Chesapeake* was attacked and boarded, and four alleged deserters were taken and impressed into service in the British Navy. However, Jefferson was able to avoid war.
In October, the Senate ratified the treaty in which the United States took control of new lands west of the Mississippi through the Louisiana Purchase.	James Madison took office after Jefferson and was eventually forced into the War of 1812, even though the nation was unprepared and the Federalists in the House would vote no.
Some younger men from the southern and western states who were in favor of war with the Indians, and thus known as the "War Hawks," were elected to Congress in November 1811.	The United States ended the war with Tripoli in 1815 by getting the ruler to sign a treaty promising to let American ships alone without the payment of a bribe.
Lewis and Clark reached the Pacific Ocean after starting up the Missouri River from St. Louis on a two-year journey in which they mapped and studied the newly acquired Louisiana Purchase.	Aaron Burr fatally wounded Alexander Hamilton in a duel. Hamilton had declared that Burr was not to be trusted with the reins of government when he heard of a scheme to make New York and New Jersey an independent confederacy.

Make a Time Line

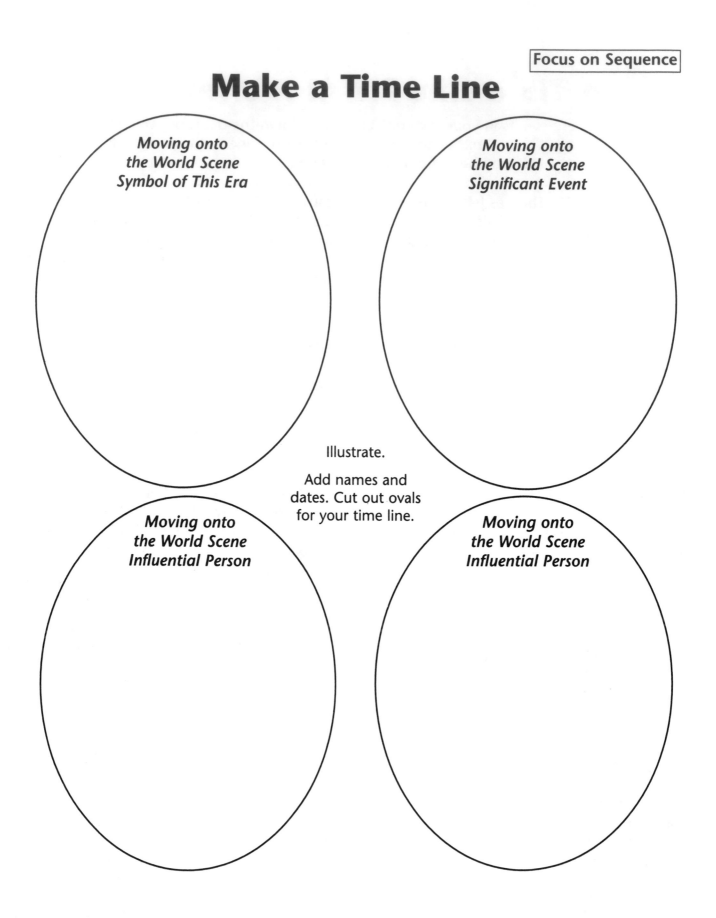

*Moving onto
the World Scene
Symbol of This Era*

*Moving onto
the World Scene
Significant Event*

Illustrate.

Add names and
dates. Cut out ovals
for your time line.

*Moving onto
the World Scene
Influential Person*

*Moving onto
the World Scene
Influential Person*

Movement Toward Reform

The word that best describes the United States in the half century before the Civil War is *ferment*—a term which means to be excited or agitated. Everything was changing, including people's ideas. There were new inventions that were altering the way people lived and did business. Reformers were seeking to improve almost everything about society. Writers were preaching faith in democracy and the individual, while painters were capturing the rural and optimistic spirit of the times.

This was a religious age that was moving toward emphasizing individual relationships to God. As religious belief was often carried into action, it was a time of religious revivals and calls for revisions in the everyday world. It was a time for building more schools and improving conditions for the helpless. In a sense, it was a time of innocence, when everyday Americans believed they could build a more perfect society.

No one represents the belief in social and political reform better than Henry David Thoreau and his friend Ralph Waldo Emerson. They and many others like them turned their backs on conventional ways. They encouraged people to reevaluate what was important in life. Painting at mid-century also reflected these same ideals. Artists like Asher Durand and Frederic Church of the Hudson River School painted scenes untouched by civilization. Others, like George Catlin, set out for the West to paint the wild land and the quickly changing world of the Indian.

Those in the movement to end slavery were becoming more and more vocal, as were advocates for women's rights. Some reformers called for better schools, others for more humane treatment of the mentally ill. This nation was thriving, not only because it had gifted writers, leaders with vision, and inventors with genius, but also because it had ordinary people who became reformers and educators. These were folks who cared enough about their fellow human beings to see that social injustices were attacked. It is no wonder that this era from 1820 to 1860 is often called the American Renaissance—the rebirth of America.

Just for Teachers

Background Information

During the years that followed the War of 1812, Americans wanted their nation to be strong and independent of the rest of the world. A national bank, high tariffs, and an east-west transportation system helped to make the United States economically independent and self-sufficient. Educators, artists, and writers devoted their efforts to American themes and heroes. Their efforts helped make the United States culturally as well as politically independent of Europe.

The Industrial Revolution caused the growth of cities in the East and Middle West and textile mills in the South. It provided people with new and different ways of earning a living and put money in their pockets to buy goods and raise their standard of living. Immigrants found jobs in railroad building, industry, and farming. But industrialism also created new problems as wage earners came into conflict with owners, and serious differences between the industrial North and the agrarian South intensified.

As this tempo of change within the culture increased, great pressure was exerted on ways of perceiving, thinking, feeling, and acting, both among individuals and among social groups. In order to understand this American Renaissance, students need to consider pictures, read short biographies, sample literature, and in general take a look at the various cultural and reform movements of the 1820s, 1830s, and 1840s that set the scene for the Civil War.

Student pages

| Focus on Skills | *American Renaissance—Folders and Cognitive Map* |

In order to do the cognitive map activity, the teacher will need to prepare a minimum of ten folders with pictures, biographies, paragraphs, and other material from the American Renaissance and the Second Great Awakening in the 1820s, 1830s, and 1840s. These folders can be used by groups of three or four students and passed among groups. Most of the material can be cut from one or two out-of-use textbooks. Since many colored prints of famous paintings are often found without emphasizing the painter or the cultural milieu, grouping them together will provide a better focus. Include only one theme or topic in each folder. Samples might be Abolitionists, Artists of The Hudson Valley School, Reform in Education, Women's Concerns, Americana in Art, The Flowering of American Literature, Frontier Artists, Poems and Poets, Inventions and Inventors, Helping the Downtrodden. Be certain there is enough information in the folders that students can cover the subjects of painting, literature, women's concerns, abolition, and education. Paste a copy of the American Renaissance cognitive map on the back of each folder. This sheet should also be duplicated for each student.

Each group will receive one folder to use to complete the cognitive map. When the group has finished with one folder, it can be exchanged for another. There may be enough duplication of information between folders so that every group need not have seen every folder. Although students will be working in groups and helping one another interpret the information in the folders, each student should be responsible for completing his or her own cognitive map.

Focus on Research | *American Renaissance—Finding Quiz Answers*

The format for this invitation to research is a multiple-choice quiz. Students should take the quiz and then find the answers in their books or encyclopedia.

Focus on Maps | *Who Worked Where?*

It is useful for students to learn to place people and events on maps, because many students believe maps can show only physical features or stationary landmarks. On this map of the United States, students locate the homes of some of the reformers and inventors who were active in the American Renaissance. Research can be done in encyclopedias and biographical dictionaries. Students show where at least five were born and where they moved in order to carry on their life's work. On the line, they are to write something about the person's contribution. Suggestions are: John Deere (Massachusetts to Illinois), Bronson Alcott (Massachusetts to New York), Dorothea Dix (Maine to Washington, D.C.), Angelina Grimke (South Carolina to Pennsylvania), Susan B. Anthony (Massachusetts to New York), Cyrus McCormick (Virginia to Illinois), Harriet Tubman (Maryland to New York).

Focus on Writing | *Writing Multiple-Choice Questions*

When the cognitive maps are complete, each group should then write three or more multiple-choice questions to ask the rest of the class. These can be used at the end of the period or for a review the following day. A sample question is provided on the page along with a place for students to record answers to other students' questions.

Hands-on Activity | *American Renaissance Wall Hanging*

Duplicate the activity sheet on colored paper. In each panel, students write a descriptive phrase about one component of the American Renaissance. Then, they cut out the panels and glue them back to back. Holes are to be punched on each side at the top and bottom and the panels strung together on two pieces of colored yarn. Pairs of students can put their panels together.

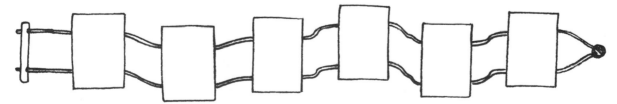

Focus on Sequence | *Make a Time Line*

This section ends with a time line page. Directions for making a fan-fold time line booklet are given in "The Explorers Move Out" section.

American Renaissance— Folders and Cognitive Map

During the first half of the nineteenth century, there was a quickening of interest in literature, music, art, and the social conscience. As you look at the material supplied, fill in and add to the cognitive map to help you remember some of the things that were going on.

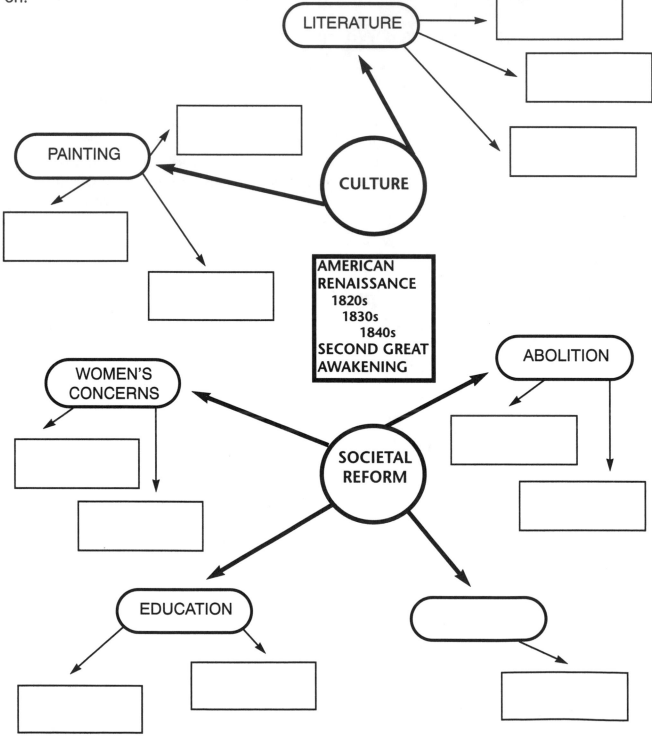

American Renaissance—
Finding Quiz Answers

You are not expected to know the answers to these questions when you begin. Go through the quiz and answer any items that you already know. Then, use your textbook to find the answers to the others. This is a way of researching to find specific data. The index at the back of your book should prove helpful.

1. During the period of the American Renaissance in Literature, who was known as "Preacher to the World"?
   A. Ralph Waldo Emerson   B. Henry David Thoreau
   C. Edgar Allan Poe   D. Horace Mann

2. During the period of the American Renaissance and the Second Great Awakening, education was the main concern of:
   A. Ralph Waldo Emerson   B. Henry David Thoreau
   C. Edgar Allan Poe   D. Horace Mann

3. During the period of the Second Great Awakening, who was a famous reformer who helped with the mentally ill?
   A. Frederick Douglass   B. Dorothea Dix
   C. Horace Mann   D. Elizabeth Cady Stanton

4. When was the period of the American Renaissance of writing and painting?
   A. late 1700s   B. mid 1800s
   C. late 1800s   D. early 1900s

5. What was the Underground Railroad?
   A. The beginnings of the modern transit system
   B. A place where kids hung out and drank
   C. A music group of the American Renaissance
   D. A system of houses and safe places for slaves

6. During the early nineteenth century, a unique style of painting was developed known as:
   A. Hudson Bay Company   B. Impressionists
   C. Hudson River Valley School D. Big River School

7. Two women who saw and spoke out against the horrors of slavery were
   A. Mary Williams and Joyce Mayflower
   B. Susan B. Anthony and Elizabeth Cady Stanton
   C. Emma Willard and Dorothea Dix
   D. Angelina and Sarah Grimke

8. A writer from this period, whose "Civil Disobedience" had impact on later generations:
   A. Ralph Waldo Emerson   B. Henry David Thoreau
   C. John Greenleaf Whittier   D. Henry Wadsworth Longfellow

Who Worked Where?

Even in the early 1800s, many people moved in order to carry on their life's work. During the first half of the century all of these reformers or inventors moved from the state where they were born: John Deere, Bronson Alcott, Dorothea Dix, Angelina Grimke, Susan B. Anthony, Cyrus McCormick, Harriet Tubman. On the map below, show the move that at least five of these people made, and include the name of the person. On the line, write something about the contribution of each. Place the initials of each person in front of his or her contribution.

1. _____

2. _____

3. _____

4. _____

5. _____

6. _____

7. _____

Writing Multiple-Choice Questions

After you have filled in your Content Map, write three multiple-choice questions to ask the rest of the class. Sample:

Abolitionist Sarah Grimke had a sister named
A. Susan   B. Mary
C. Angelina   D. Emma

1. _____

_____

_____

A. _____

B. _____

C. _____

D. _____

2. _____

_____

_____

A. _____

B. _____

C. _____

D. _____

3. _____

_____

_____

A. _____

B. _____

C. _____

D. _____

Here is a place to write the answers to questions asked by your classmates.

1. _____ 2. _____ 3. _____ 4. _____ 5. _____ 6. _____ 7. _____

8. _____ 9. _____ 10. _____ 11. _____ 12. _____ 13. _____ 14. _____

15. _____ 16. _____ 17. _____ 18. _____ 19. _____ 20. _____

Score: _____

American Renaissance Wall Hanging

In each of the rectangles below, write a phrase that describes some aspect of the American Renaissance. Illustrate the phrase. Cut out the panels and glue them back to back. Punch a hole on each side at the top and bottom. String the panels together with pieces of colored yarn. The first one is done for you.

AMERICAN RENAISSANCE

Harriet Beecher Stowe wrote Uncle Tom's Cabin

AMERICAN RENAISSANCE

AMERICAN RENAISSANCE

AMERICAN RENAISSANCE

AMERICAN RENAISSANCE

AMERICAN RENAISSANCE

Make a Time Line

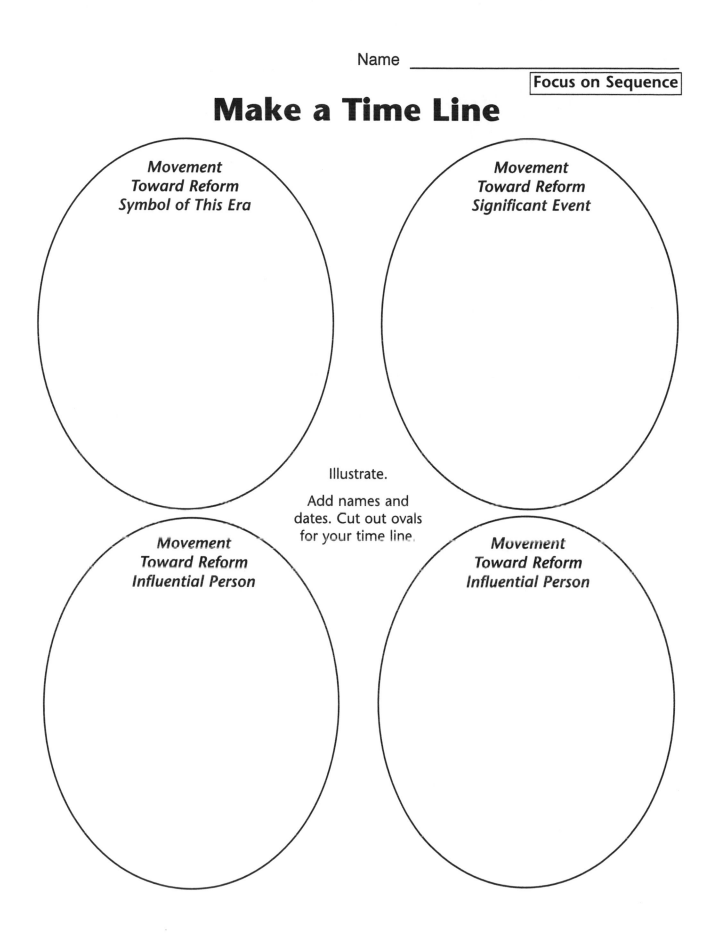

*Movement
Toward Reform
Symbol of This Era*

*Movement
Toward Reform
Significant Event*

Illustrate.

Add names and
dates. Cut out ovals
for your time line.

*Movement
Toward Reform
Influential Person*

*Movement
Toward Reform
Influential Person*

Moving West—the Old Frontier

Once the new nation was established, people turned westward during the nineteenth century to expand the national boundaries. Settlers moved beyond the Appalachians toward the Mississippi River and then farther west to the Missouri River and the Rocky Mountains.

By 1827, the railroads opened a new era in transportation. Ten years later they were carrying freight all over the country. And all of this new land was in demand, because by 1850 the United States had grown from a population of 4 million to a population of 23 million.

At about the same time that the Civil War began, enterprising Americans decided that the Great Plains could be used for raising beef cattle. Much of this land soon became open range over which cowboys drove vast herds of cattle to railroad shipping points. Along these cattle trails, rowdy western towns began to develop. Within 50 years, this huge area of plains and plateaus was settled, organized into states, and admitted to the Union.

When gold was discovered in California in 1849, and in Colorado in 1859, the rush westward intensified. Many of those who came to find their fortune stayed to take up steadier ways of making a living. The wagon trains continued to move west when the Homestead Act of 1862 provided free land to citizens interested in crop farming. This act brought many pioneer families to the West and led to conflicts between ranchers and farmers. On the frontier, the desire to work, ambition, initiative, kindliness, courage, and persistence—rather than his family and social connections—became the measure of a man's worth.

Just for Teachers

Background Information

Americans were thrilled by the vision of a country that extended across the entire continent. This desire was justified by a New York newspaperman, John L. O'Sullivan, who said it was "our manifest destiny to overspread and to possess the whole continent which Providence has given us for the development of the great experiment of liberty and federated self-government entrusted to us."

After the passage of the Homestead Act in 1862, settlers poured into the western prairies and plains in great numbers. The number of settlers was so great that the original inhabitants, the Indians, were forced off the land and onto reservations.

Each of the three groups of settlers—cattlemen, farmers, and miners—made use of the grasslands, the fertile soil, or precious metals as a resource. Although these were real people with real lives, many myths grew up about them. In reality, the cowboys lived a hard and lonely life on the open range, where they tended and moved their cattle. When the farmers moved in with barbed wire fencing and tools that let them utilize the dry land, the cowboys began to disappear. The miners, too, had a few years of glory and then settled into more ordinary pursuits.

Each person's view of the past is influenced by the availability of evidence of what was happening at the time. Understanding the forces and conflicts that influenced the change that was taking place may be greatly enhanced by taking a look at some of the objects that the people used in their daily lives.

Student pages

Focus on Research *Major Events in the Westward Movement*

> Place students in groups and have them use their books and notes to make a list of 20 or more of the major events of the 1800s Manifest Destiny era. Each event is then written on one flag on the "Manifest Destiny Play Dough Map" activity sheet. More than one sheet will be needed by the group. Afterwards, the flags should be folded and glued to toothpicks. A minimum of 15 toothpicks should be prepared. (Examples: Louisiana Purchase in 1803, Texas annexation in 1845, Mormons settling Utah in 1847, California gold rush in 1849, Gadsden Purchase in 1853, Colorado gold rush in 1859)

Classifying Primary Source Artifacts

Students will look at the drawings of primary source artifacts and classify them on a chart, deciding whether each object was used by a cowboy, a farmer, or a miner. The drawings include such things as a butter churn and spurs. You may wish to supplement the drawings with a few actual examples or photographs, if they are available. It is important to explain to students that the drawings are not really primary sources but merely representations of objects that might be found in a museum. This lesson will help students understand how curators decide how to group the objects in their collections.

Focus on Maps *Manifest Destiny Practice Map*

Students will use the list of major events of the Manifest Destiny era prepared in the research activity to locate specific areas affected by the events. Since this map is relatively small, students may use the numbers from their list rather than write in all of the words. They will then use this map as a plan for making the play dough map of the hands-on activity. Before beginning to identify locations, they should color the Mississippi River, the Great Lakes, and the Appalachian and Rocky Mountains.

Hands-on Activity *Manifest Destiny Play Dough Map*

To make play dough maps, prepare bowls of green, brown, blue, and white play dough (2 cups flour, 1 cup salt, 1 cup water, ⅛ cup oil, ¼ tsp. alum, drops of food coloring). Often, students are willing to prepare the play dough and bring it to class. Duplicate flag outlines. Cut out several outline maps of the United States (to be shared). Each group will need a piece of cardboard cut from boxes as a work surface covered with plastic wrap or waxed paper. Each group will also need a paper plate and a plastic spoon. It is suggested that the U.S. map be enlarged on the copier to fit an 11" x 17" sheet of paper so it is large enough to be worked on by groups.

Students use the list of various events of the Manifest Destiny era and then represent them on a relief map of their own making. The completed activity sheets from the research and practice map activities will be useful as working models. Information from the research sheet is to be transferred to the diamond-shaped flags. The flags are then cut out, folded in half, and glued to the top of a toothpick. This should be done a day before starting the play dough map. The flags can be stored in an envelope.

While some of the group members are preparing the work surface and tracing and cutting a poster board map, others should mix different colors of play dough on a paper plate. Play dough is to be used to cover the entire surface of the outline map. Color coding can be of the students' choosing. Mountain ranges should be shown as well as major rivers. Use colored markers to accent the landforms. After the map is finished but before it is dry, toothpick flags should be placed at the appropriate locations. Little bits of play dough may be needed to help make bases for the toothpicks.

Focus on Writing | *The Journey West*

Each student chooses one object shown on the Primary Sources sheet and tells its history. The story should be written from the perspective of the object. The student can tell where it began, who made it, and why it began the journey west. The story continues with some of its adventures and finishes with its situation today. The activity sheet provides for a single episode story—one which would be useful for sharing with younger children.

Focus on Sequence | *Make a Time Line*

This section ends with a time line page. Directions for making a fan-fold time line booklet are given in "The Explorers Move Out" section.

Major Events in the Westward Movement

Make a list of at least 20 of the many events in the westward movement influenced by the American belief in Manifest Destiny. (Examples: Louisiana Purchase in 1803, Texas annexation in 1845, Mormons settling Utah in 1847, California gold rush in 1849, Gadsden Purchase in 1853, Colorado gold rush in 1859). Write the dates of the events in the blanks on the right side of the page. You will use this list for both the mapping and the hands-on activities.

1. _____ _____

2. _____ _____

3. _____ _____

4. _____ _____

5. _____ _____

6. _____ _____

7. _____ _____

8. _____ _____

9. _____ _____

10. _____ _____

11. _____ _____

12. _____ _____

13. _____ _____

14. _____ _____

15. _____ _____

16. _____ _____

17. _____ _____

18. _____ _____

19. _____ _____

20. _____ _____

21. _____ _____

22. _____ _____

23. _____ _____

24. _____ _____

Classifying Primary Source Artifacts

Research some of the artifacts used by cattlemen, farmers, and miners in the Old West, inferring how they might have been used and by whom. Design a chart similar to the one below, using the drawings of primary source artifacts as well as any materials provided by your teacher, items from the textbook, or objects you have seen in museums. Be ready to answer these questions: What can you tell about this object? How old is it? How do you think it was used and by whom? Which group used this object?

Artifact	Who Used It	For What

Manifest Destiny Practice Map

Review the map of the United States below. Add markers for the events you listed in your research. Numbers can be written on the map and the list used as the legend to identify the events. This map can be used as a plan for a play dough map.

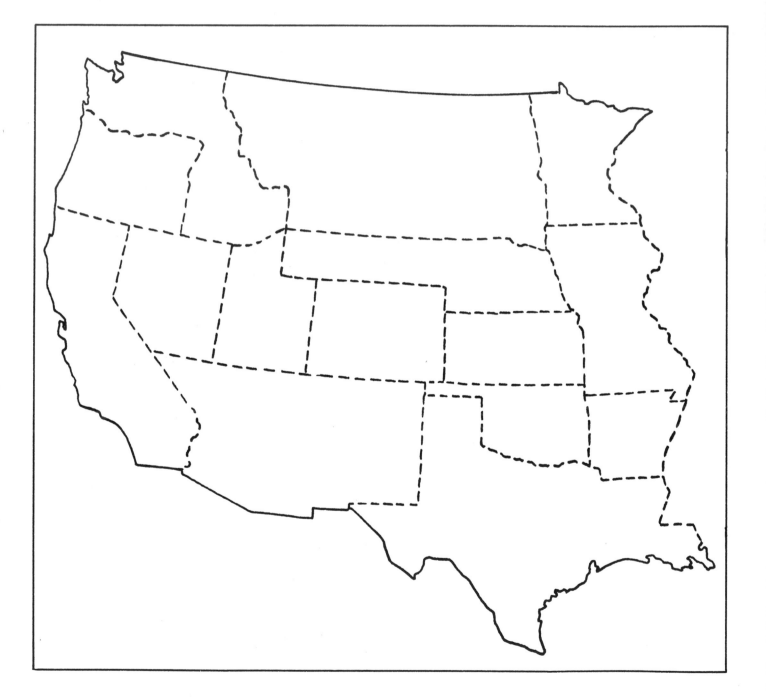

Manifest Destiny Play Dough Map

Each group will need a cardboard work surface (plastic wrap or wax paper), to cover the surface, a piece of poster board, and a poster board outline map of the United States to trace. Some students will prepare the work surface, tracing and cutting a poster board map while others mix different colors of play dough on a paper plate. You will need to cover the entire surface of the outline map with dough. Color coding can be of your own choosing. Colored markers can be used to accent certain features. After the map is finished but before it is dry, toothpick flags should be placed at the appropriate locations. The diamond shapes have to be cut out, folded in two, and glued around a toothpick. Little bits of play dough may be needed to help make bases for the toothpicks.

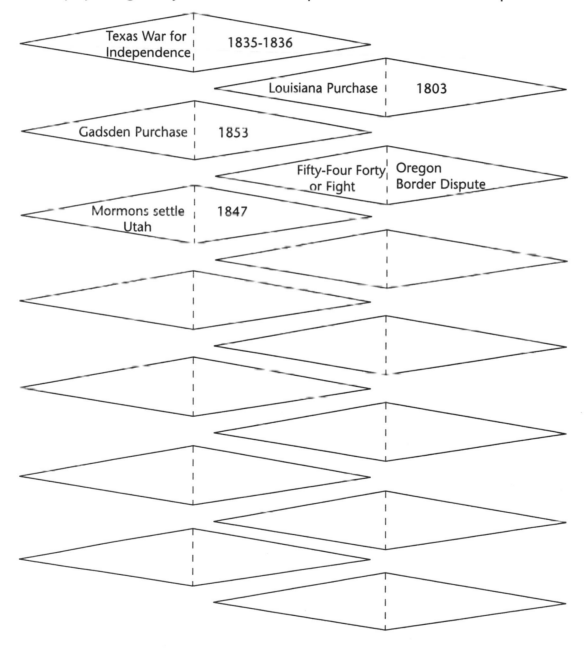

The Journey West

Choose one drawing from the "Classifying Primary Source Artifacts" sheet. Tell the story of this object, from its point of view. You can explain how the journey west began and about adventures along the way. To have a good story, your object should want something (a goal). The story finishes with the goal met or not met and the feelings of the object.

1. Introduce your object as the main character. Tell about where the story begins.

_____
_____
_____
_____

2. Tell about some action that caused your object to have a goal. Explain what it wanted.

_____
_____
_____
_____

3. Explain the feelings and thoughts of the object that cause it to start doing something.

_____
_____
_____
_____

4. Tell what happens as the object tries to meet its goal.

_____
_____
_____
_____

5. Tell of an event whereby the object is able or not able to fulfill its goal.

_____
_____
_____
_____

6. Explain how the object feels about the outcome.

_____
_____
_____

Make a Time Line

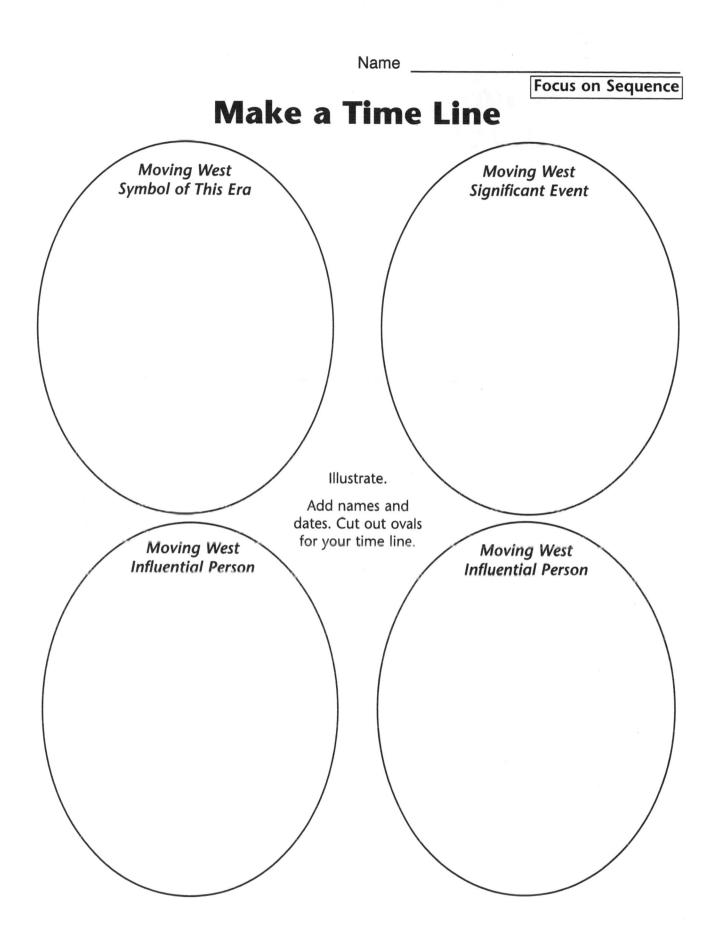

Moving West
Symbol of This Era

Moving West
Significant Event

Illustrate.

Add names and
dates. Cut out ovals
for your time line.

Moving West
Influential Person

Moving West
Influential Person

Moving Toward Restructuring

The Civil War was a terrible time for this country. It was a time when brother fought brother, when mothers lost sons, and wives lost husbands. It was a time of heroes and heroines on both sides of the battle lines. It was a time when places like Gettysburg and Antietam and Manassas would become never-forgotten markers on the landscape of America. Only after the end of the war could the nation get on with the business of moving forward.

After the slaughter was over, the Southern states began a time of reconstructing their way of living. The process brought forth argument after argument over the constitutional powers of the federal government. Many in Congress were determined to make fundamental changes in the South. Former officials and military officers were denied the right to vote. So-called carpetbaggers arrived from the North to take advantage of this unrest. Reconstruction left a nasty legacy to future generations of Americans. White Southerners felt deeply wronged and created a system of segregation that kept black Americans from taking advantage of basic rights. It resulted in racial hostilities and discrimination that persist to this day.

With this upheaval, the freed slaves found that there were still many things that kept them from achieving the American dream. Education seemed to hold one answer. As time went on, three men became leaders in the movement to educate their race. W. E. B. DuBois, Booker T. Washington, and George Washington Carver had very different ideas about the meaning of this restructuring of lives.

Just for Teachers

Background Information

Wars are made up of many battles involving many people and costing a great deal in destruction and suffering. Unfortunately, the ending of hostilities rarely means that problems are solved. The battles are only representative of deeper conflicts within a society.

What was behind the North and South going to war in 1861? Certainly slavery was not the only issue. States' rights was undoubtedly a rallying point. But most thoughtful historians cite a number of factors that must be considered. There were basic economic and social differences between the two regions which led to disagreements over tariffs, money and banking, public improvements, and the disposal of public lands. But whatever the reasons for conflict, the nation faced a formidable array of problems as it began to reunite.

Through all time and among all groups, people have worked to meet basic human needs and to satisfy human desires and aspirations. This was true at the conclusion of the Civil War. Problems arose when the aspirations of white Northerners, white Southerners, and African Americans came into conflict. Southern Blacks were faced with the challenges of finding employment, setting up households, getting an education, and taking part in the political process. While the radical republicans were mainly interested in punishing the South, all Southerners were concerned with rebuilding their economy by turning to crops other than King Cotton. Unfortunately, the bitterness and fear of white Southerners were such that they perpetuated the societal divisions epitomized by the Ku Klux Klan.

Student pages

Focus on Team Research | *Battles of the Civil War*

Have students create a small study book on important battles of the Civil War, telling when and where they occurred, their significance, and one important participant in each. Explain that you are going to show them how to help one another make something to help them remember the major events of the Civil War. Each group of students will find information on one battle of the Civil War. Each individual will create an eight-page booklet in which to record information reported by each group. Before beginning the team research, have each student fold a booklet.

Eight-page booklet

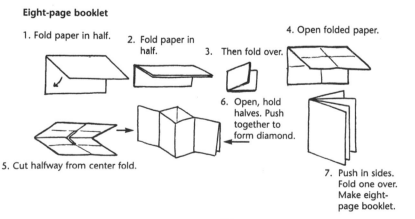

1. Fold paper in half.
2. Fold paper in half.
3. Then fold over.
4. Open folded paper.
5. Cut halfway from center fold.
6. Open, hold halves. Push together to form diamond.
7. Push in sides. Fold one over. Make eight-page booklet.

Cut up the slips on the eight major battles of the Civil War so that groups can make a random selection. On each slip, write the page number in your textbook where the information can be found.

Focus on Maps | *Reconstruction—A Problem for the States of the Confederacy*

On the map, students draw the Mason Dixon line and color the states of the Confederacy gray and the Union blue. Direct students to draw events of Reconstruction such as carpetbaggers moving south or lynching of blacks. Pictures and words can surround the map, with arrows to show location.

Focus on Learning | *Education of African Americans*

Students identify three African-American leaders who, working in very separate ways, made contributions to education in general and the welfare of African Americans in particular. Speak about the contributions of each of these men in higher education, in science, and in the political arena. Stress the differences in outlook of the three men— one who emphasized getting along and getting good jobs, one who just wanted to use knowledge to make life better, and one who insisted on equality of opportunity. Relate this information to events of the times in which they lived as well as the education and welfare of African Americans.

Focus on Skills | *Make an Every Pupil Response Card*

Read randomly from the statements about the African-American educators from the "Education of African Americans" activity page. Using Every Pupil Response Cards, have students signal which of the three people you are describing. This is a good way to review for a test as well as to emphasize the skill of categorization.

A. Washington
B. Carver
C. Du Bois

Pupil Card

A	B
C	

Front   Back

Focus on Writing | *African-American Educator Anagram*

Anagrams use the letters of a word written in one direction to suggest other words on a given topic. Have students make an anagram using the initials and last name of an important African-American educator. A sample anagram is done for them.

Focus on Sequence | *Make a Time Line*

This section ends with a time line page. Directions for making a fan-fold time line booklet are given in "The Explorers Move Out" section.

Battles of the Civil War

In groups, locate and organize information on the major events of the Civil War.
First, you need to create a booklet.

1. Fold paper in half with a short fold (horizontal fold).
2. Open up and fold each end to the center fold.
3. Open up and fold long ways (vertical fold).
4. Refold short way and cut or tear from center fold to quarter fold—the cut will be in center half of the paper.
5. Refold the long way and push ends together making an empty diamond.
6. Continue pushing together until the folded sides make a cross.
7. Fold over into double-sided eight-page book.
8. On each of the eight pages, place the following titles: Fort Sumter, First Bull Run/ Manassas, *Monitor* and *Merrimac,* Antietam, Gettysburg, Vicksburg, Sherman's March, Appomattox.

Eight-page booklet

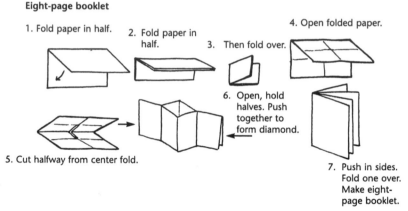

1. Fold paper in half.
2. Fold paper in half.
3. Then fold over.
4. Open folded paper.
5. Cut halfway from center fold.
6. Open, hold halves. Push together to form diamond.
7. Push in sides. Fold one over. Make eight-page booklet.

Each of the eight groups is to research and report on one of the battles. Divide up the work, find the following information, and record it here:

Battle _____

When _____

Where _____

Significance_____

_____

Important Person or Event _____

_____

As the group reports are given, write information about each event on the designated page of the booklet. This booklet then becomes your personal record of research.

Fort Sumter   Page _____

- -

First Bull Run/Manassas   Page _____

- -

Monitor and *Merrimac*   Page _____

- -

Antietam   Page _____

- -

Gettysburg   Page _____

- -

Vicksburg   Page _____

- -

Sherman's March   Page _____

- -

Appomattox   Page _____

Reconstruction—A Problem for the States of the Confederacy

On the map below, color the states of the Confederacy gray and the Union blue. It was in the states of the Confederacy where a great deal of restructuring of society took place. This reconstruction affected the lives of people socially, economically, and politically. Across the Southern states, write selected specific events of Reconstruction such as carpet baggers moving to the South, throwing out Southern state governments, denying the vote to former Confederate officials, forming the Ku Klux Klan, blacks running for office, cotton industry recovering, sharecropping started, or landowners sinking into debt.

Education of African Americans

These three African-American leaders, working in very separate ways, made contributions to education in general and the welfare of African Americans in particular. You will use this information to create an anagram, and you will need to know it before answering with the Every Pupil Response Cards.

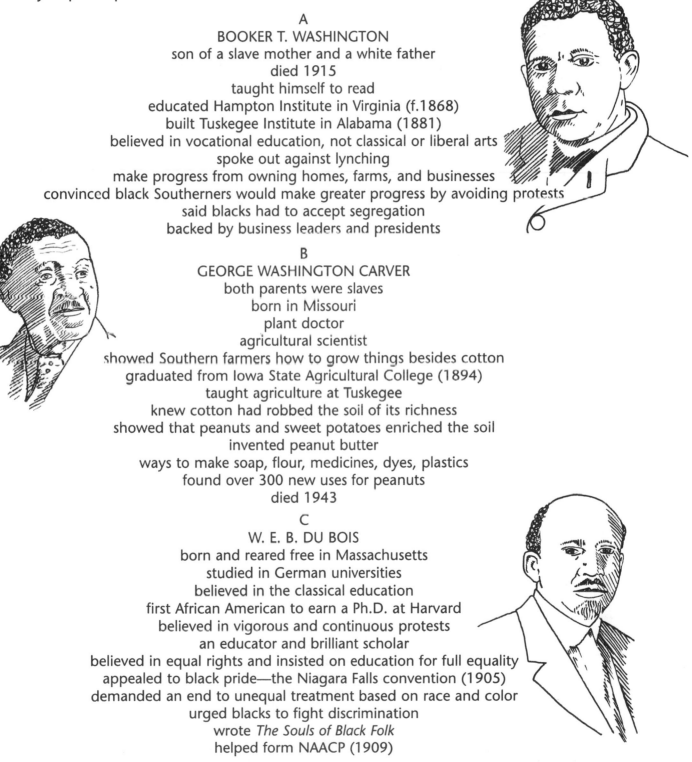

A
BOOKER T. WASHINGTON
son of a slave mother and a white father
died 1915
taught himself to read
educated Hampton Institute in Virginia (f.1868)
built Tuskegee Institute in Alabama (1881)
believed in vocational education, not classical or liberal arts
spoke out against lynching
make progress from owning homes, farms, and businesses
convinced black Southerners would make greater progress by avoiding protests
said blacks had to accept segregation
backed by business leaders and presidents

B
GEORGE WASHINGTON CARVER
both parents were slaves
born in Missouri
plant doctor
agricultural scientist
showed Southern farmers how to grow things besides cotton
graduated from Iowa State Agricultural College (1894)
taught agriculture at Tuskegee
knew cotton had robbed the soil of its richness
showed that peanuts and sweet potatoes enriched the soil
invented peanut butter
ways to make soap, flour, medicines, dyes, plastics
found over 300 new uses for peanuts
died 1943

C
W. E. B. DU BOIS
born and reared free in Massachusetts
studied in German universities
believed in the classical education
first African American to earn a Ph.D. at Harvard
believed in vigorous and continuous protests
an educator and brilliant scholar
believed in equal rights and insisted on education for full equality
appealed to black pride—the Niagara Falls convention (1905)
demanded an end to unequal treatment based on race and color
urged blacks to fight discrimination
wrote *The Souls of Black Folk*
helped form NAACP (1909)

Make an Every Pupil Response Card

Cut out the rectangle below. Fold in half longwise with the letters showing. Glue sides together. Use this response card to show which of the three African-American educators is being described by the statement read by the teacher. In this way you are practicing categorizing descriptive phrases.

A. Washington
B. Carver
C. Du Bois

Pupil Card

A B

Ɔ

Front   Back

African-American Educator Anagram

Anagrams use the letters of a word written in one direction to suggest other words on a given topic. A sample anagram is done for you.

```
sTrict
friEndly
hAppy
 Caring
 Helpful
enErgetic
tRusted
```

Choose one of the three African-American educators discussed and write the letters of his name vertically. Then write descriptors about that person.

Make a Time Line

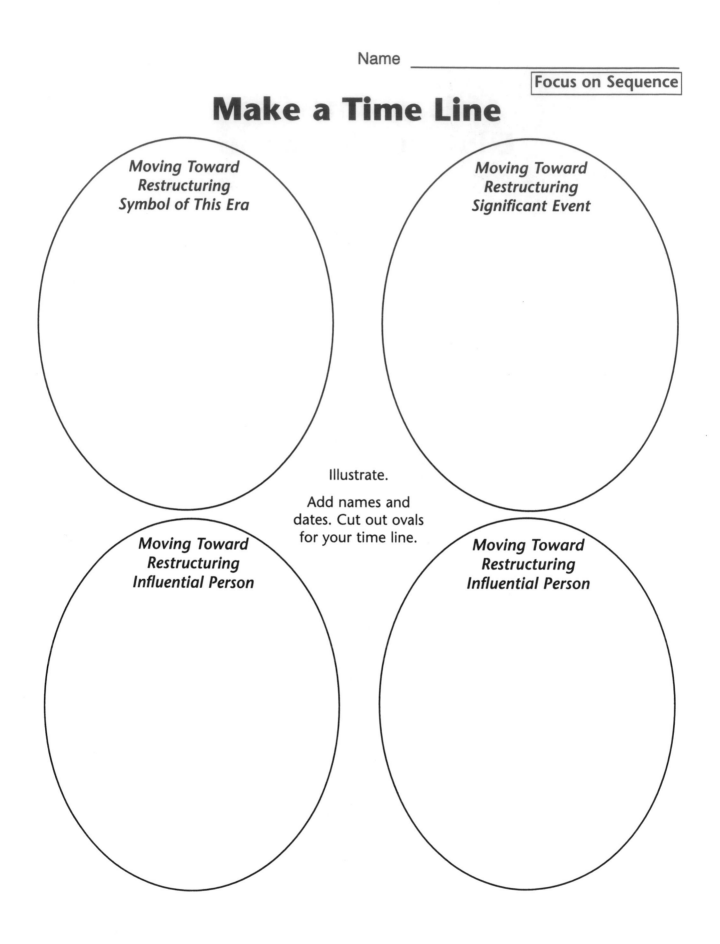

*Moving Toward
Restructuring
Symbol of This Era*

*Moving Toward
Restructuring
Significant Event*

Illustrate.

Add names and
dates. Cut out ovals
for your time line.

*Moving Toward
Restructuring
Influential Person*

*Moving Toward
Restructuring
Influential Person*

Moving Toward Industrialization

The expansion of industry after 1865 affected almost every product imaginable. But it was the new industries that were the basis for the enormous industrial growth of the United States. Men like Andrew Carnegie saw the potential of a new method of removing impurities from melted iron and founded great fortunes from the growth of steel production. John D. Rockefeller, who recognized the growing importance of petroleum, realized that there was more profit in refining oil than in producing it. His huge fortune, like that of financier J. P. Morgan, came from devising ways to eliminate competition through ruthless business practices.

This period from 1865 to 1900 was a time of business prosperity, political corruption, declining farm prices, and great extremes of wealth and poverty. Money did the talking in all facets of life. Wealth was concentrated in the hands of the powerful industrialists and railroad magnates. They influenced elections, bribed politicians, and caused government intervention in their behalf.

Cities grew rapidly because workers moved there for the new jobs that were being created. Growth in the large mail-order houses brought city goods to country customers. The storekeeper could stay in the big city, where it was easier to have a large stock of goods, and send them by mail to people who would appreciate the quality customer service.

As the industries grew, work changed. Unskilled factory workers, unlike farmers, were scorned and looked down upon. Working conditions were unsafe, causing disease and loss of life and limb. All this gave rise to the growth of labor unions and strikes marked by violence and bitterness.

89

Just for Teachers

Background Information

With the expansion of industry came the development of new cities and the rapid growth of older ones. But without advances in science and technology, these large industrial cities would not have been possible. Countless numbers of inventions and discoveries drove the changes that were taking place in all aspects of American life—from education to architecture, from recreation to journalism.

Industrialization increased the demand for skilled and unskilled labor. The jobs created provided people with more money to spend on "luxuries." But business practices also prompted the growth of the labor union movement and inevitable conflicts with management.

The increased productivity, brought about by mass-production techniques, led to the need for new markets and the growth of practices to entice consumers. Some businesses went nationwide to get customers, thus making them very wealthy and powerful. Things were changing with bewildering speed, and everyone had to adjust their lives to the new conditions. But many problems still had to be solved.

Student pages

Focus on Research | *Promoting a New Consumerism*

Have students bring ads for clothing or household items from a newspaper or magazine. Have them compare these ads with the ads from a May 1886 issue of the *New York Times* or an old Sears Roebuck catalog, available at most libraries. Ask students how advertisements are a reflection of the times in which they are published. Students are to use ads to answer the questions on the "Promoting a New Consumerism" sheet.

Focus on Skills | *Industrialization Brings Change*

Students analyze the effects of industrialization on the lives of the people in different social classes. They must first use textbooks to make a list of the changes in American lifestyles during this period. The changes are entered in the data retrieval chart, depending on whether they most affected the upper, middle, or lower classes. After deciding who was affected by the change, students complete the chart by telling why they were affected and how they reacted to the change.

Focus on Thinking | *Understanding Analogical Reasoning*

Explain analogies to students as a way of finding relationships between words. Inform them that this type of reasoning is being used on this sheet to consider people, institutions, and technology from the late 1800s. Mention that analogies are read "black is to white as up is to down." Present to students these eight different types of analogical relationships. Show them the chart. Afterwards, have students solve the analogies on the activity sheet which you have prepared by whiting out one word. If they make analogy matching cards, they can continue to practice the skill.

Classification	Analogy	What to Think
1. Word meaning	short : tall	same, different
2. Class member	rose : flower	kind of, are both
	scales : justice	symbol of
3. Part/whole	word : sentence	is a part of
4. Time order	boy : man	came before, after
5. Description	yellow : sun	tells about
6. Function/action	pencil : paper	used on, with, does
7. Made from	window : glass	is made of
8. Location	ceiling : wall	below, in, on, over

Focus on Writing | *Change in American Lifestyles*

In pairs, students write analogies of their own, using different types of relationships as shown on the chart. Write one analogy per box, using the format shown. In turn, pairs of students can read the first three words of one analogy they have written and call on another pair to answer. These analogies can also be used on analogy matching cards.

Focus on Review | *Graph-a-Word (Planning Sheet and Score Sheet)*

Students play Graph-a-Word using vocabulary from the textbook and lectures. A transparency of the Graph-a-Word score sheet should be prepared for the overhead projector. Present the transparency, divide students into teams, and invite them to alternately choose a set of coordinates. Referring to the hidden teacher-made graph, tell the team whether it has a hit or a miss. A hit scores one point, and the letter is written on the score sheet. A team may choose to guess a word on its turn. If correct, the team states a definition and earns five points. If incorrect, it loses three points.

Focus on Interpretation *A Cartoonist's View*

Give students the activity sheet of the two cartoon characters from this time period. Explain that one is supposed to be a millionaire robber baron and the other a politician he has bribed. One example might be J. P. Morgan and a New York senator or John D. Rockefeller and a congressman from Pennsylvania. Students are to label the figures and then write down what each might be saying. Examples might be, "Who wouldn't do a favor for a man who has a hundred million dollars?" or "Why would I run for office if I couldn't be bought?" The figures may be colored if there is time.

Hands-on Activity *Labor Begins to Organize/The Labor Movement Begins*

Using their textbooks, students decide whether the phrase on the sheet describes the Knights of Labor or the American Federation of Labor. Then, they glue or write the phrases onto the diagram and make illustrations around the edges.

Focus on Sequence *Make a Time Line*

This section ends with a time line page. Directions for making a fan-fold time line booklet are given in "The Explorers Move Out" section.

Name _____

Promoting a New Consumerism

Look at old advertisements in catalogs and newspapers from the late 1800s and early 1900s and compare them to those you see today. Record some of your observations to share with the class.

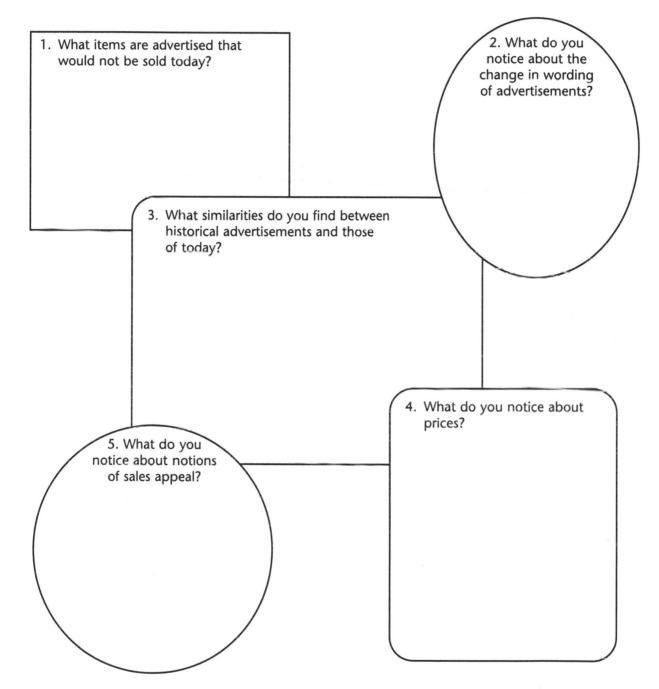

1. What items are advertised that would not be sold today?

2. What do you notice about the change in wording of advertisements?

3. What similarities do you find between historical advertisements and those of today?

4. What do you notice about prices?

5. What do you notice about notions of sales appeal?

Industrialization Brings Change

Make a list of the changes in American lifestyles during the period characterized by industrialization. Categorize and explain your list by placing each item on this chart. Indicate who was affected by the change, why they were affected, and how they reacted to the change.

DATA RETRIEVAL CHART OF CHANGES IN AMERICAN LIFESTYLES

	Change Brought About by Industrialization	Reason	Response to Change
Upper Classes			
Middle Classes			
Lower Classes			

Understanding Analogical Reasoning

Complete the analogy by writing a word in the blank. Use your textbook as a resource.

Carnegie : steel :: Rockefeller : oil

partner : partnership :: stockholder : corporation

cable : ocean floor :: telegraph wire : telegraph poles

Bell : telephone :: Edison : electric light

P. T. Barnum : circus :: Horatio Alger : stories

transportation : railroad :: communication : telephone

Pulitzer : newspapers :: Mark Twain : books

Montgomery Ward : mail order :: Hearst : press empire

railroads : pools :: oil companies : monopolies

Analogy Matching Cards

To practice using analogies, write each half of an analogy on a 3" x 5" card. You can use the analogies above, use ones you have written, or find examples in books.

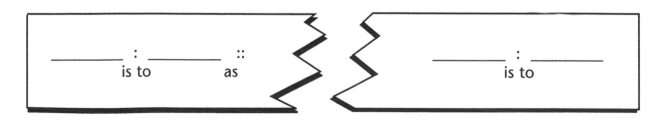

Name _____

Change in American Lifestyles

Write analogies of your own, using different types of relationships or classifications as explained by your teacher. Write one analogy per box using the format shown. When everyone is finished, be prepared to read the first three words of one analogy and to call on another student to answer.

Classification	Analogy	What to Think
1. Word meaning	short : tall	same, different
2. Class member	rose : flower	kind of, are both
	scales : justice	symbol of
3. Part/whole	word : sentence	is a part of
4. Time order	boy : man	came before, after
5. Description	yellow : sun	tells about
6. Function/action	pencil : paper	used on, with, does
7. Made from	window : glass	is made of
8. Location	ceiling : wall	below, in, on, over

1. Word meaning

_____ : _____ :: _____ : _____
means the same as   just as   means the same as

2. Class member

_____ : _____ :: _____ : _____
is a kind of   just as   is a kind of

3. Part/whole

_____ : _____ :: _____ : _____
is a part of a   just as   is a part of a

4. Time order

_____ : _____ :: _____ : _____
comes before   just as   comes before

5. Description

_____ : _____ :: _____ : _____
tells about   just as   describes

_____ : _____ :: _____ : _____
is a symbol of   just as   is a symbol of

6. Function/action

_____ : _____ :: _____ : _____
is used with   just as   goes with

7. Made from

_____ : _____ :: _____ : _____
is made from   just as   is made of

8. Location (below, in, on, over, near)

_____ : _____ :: _____ : _____
is located   just as   is located

Graph-a-Word Planning Sheet

This game is played by teams calling out coordinates at their turn. This sheet is to be used to plan the games for the whole class. See score sheet for rules.

Pairs can also play when each person has two grids (bottom half of this sheet) and fills out one for himself/herself and records hits on the other player on the second. Words must be taken from the textbook chapter. The winner is the one who captures all of the other person's words.

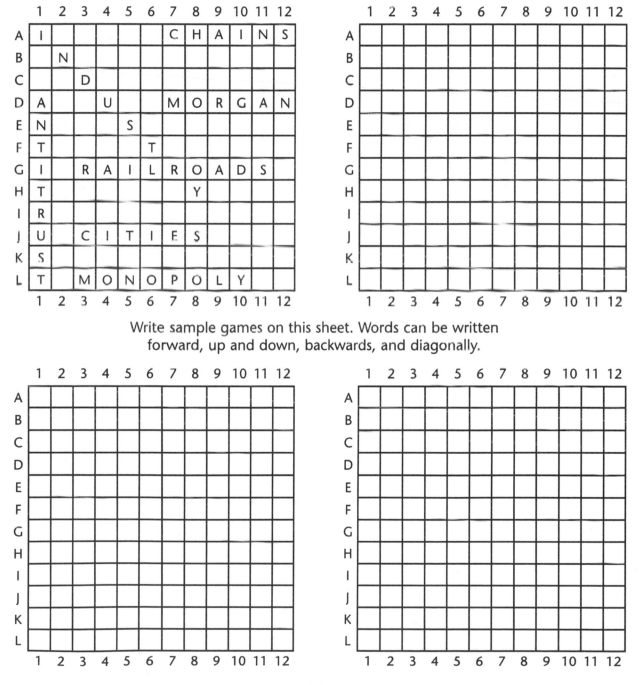

Write sample games on this sheet. Words can be written
forward, up and down, backwards, and diagonally.

Graph-a-Word Score Sheet

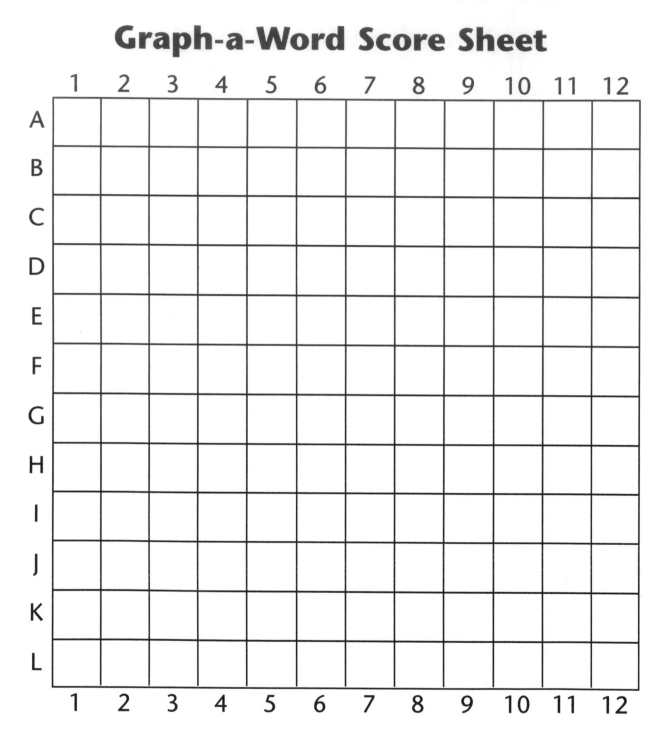

How to Play Graph-a-Word

Call out the coordinates of a space. The teacher will tell you whether it is a hit or a miss.

If it is a hit, you will be told the letter, and you score one point.

The next team calls out a new set of coordinates.

On your turn, you may guess a word rather than a letter.

If you call the word correctly, you score five points, but if you are incorrect, you lose three points.

Your teacher has already made out a sheet with all of the words.

You must keep a record of hits (letters, words) and misses.

A Cartoonist's View

Political cartoonists at this time drew attention to ruthless business practices and to the control big business had over Congress. Choose names, label the figures and then write down what they are saying.

Labor Begins to Organize

Read these phrases about the Knights of Labor and the American Federation of Labor. Then, decide on which side of the accompanying diagram to glue each phrase.

Knights of Labor

American Federation of Labor

Orientation was practical, concentrating on higher wages, shorter hours, and improved working conditions.

Organized in 1869 by the garment cutters of Philadelphia, this group was opposed to strikes.

This organization was idealistic—wanted to bring all workers together and give workers a proper share of the wealth they created.

These member unions used patriotic symbols and inspiring mottos.

As president, Terence Powderly opposed strikes, fought against child labor, and demanded the eight-hour day.

This organization had secret meetings and special handshakes.

Some members were involved in the Haymarket Riot, which caused the group to be lumped with anarchists and communists in public opinion.

Samuel Gompers was their practical and businesslike founder and go-getter organizer.

Skilled workers had to belong to a trade union first, for it was a union made up of other unions.

This organization charged high dues to establish a strike fund to pay workers who went on strike.

This organization only allowed strikes when there was enough money to hold out long enough to succeed.

At first this group was open to skilled workers only but soon came to include women, blacks, and unskilled workers.

The Labor Movement Begins

Using your textbook, decide which phrases on the "Labor Begins to Organize" sheet describe the Knights of Labor and which describe the American Federation of Labor. Glue or write the phrases onto the diagram and make illustrations around the edges.

Knights of Labor	American Federation of Labor

Make a Time Line

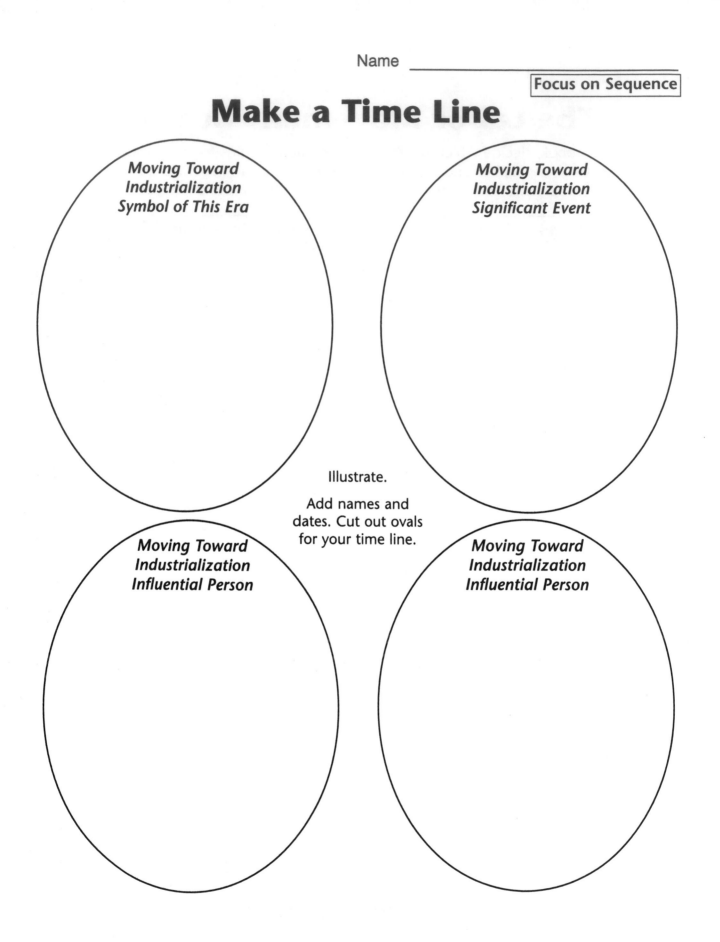

Moving Toward Industrialization Symbol of This Era

Moving Toward Industrialization Significant Event

Illustrate.

Add names and dates. Cut out ovals for your time line.

Moving Toward Industrialization Influential Person

Moving Toward Industrialization Influential Person

Moving into the Twentieth Century

In the nineteenth century, almost all Americans believed in progress. It seemed to them that the nation was improving in many ways. It was gaining territory. Its population was increasing. The nation was also growing in wealth. By the turn of the century, the United States began to reach outward as a result of rapid industrialization.

Some Americans thought things would continue to improve if government stopped interfering in the affairs of its people. But other Americans felt that the government should take an active part in shaping the nation's progress. Many people with that point of view became progressive reformers supported by writers called *muckrakers*. Using both fiction and nonfiction, they told the world about corruption in business and politics.

Around 1900, a new wave of reform began in both business and government. It was during this period that direct primaries, voter initiatives, and referendums were proposed. City governments were transformed, becoming relatively honest and efficient. Social workers labored to improve slum housing, health, and education. These reformers were so successful that the first years of the twentieth century became known as the Progressive Era.

Theodore Roosevelt and Woodrow Wilson made the office of president more important, both by promoting reforms at home and by taking an active role in foreign affairs. In 1904, the Roosevelt Corollary to the Monroe Doctrine said that the United States could intervene in the domestic affairs of Western Hemisphere nations. Just ten years later, the United States entered a European war to protect democracy against what was called German imperialism.

Just for Teachers

Background Information

During the years 1900 to 1920, the United States was transformed from an agrarian economy to an industrial economy. People saw the development of automobiles, airplanes, radios, motion pictures, and assembly lines. And the government stopped standing on the sidelines and began actively regulating the activities of business in the interest of the public welfare.

In Europe, nationalism grew and stirred up new conflicts. Ordinary citizens took pride in their own language, their national heroes, and their nation's control of faraway places. Hereditary rulers of these nations, who were all related to one another, added their own family jealousies and loyalties to all the other reasons for peace or war.

Wars have multiple causes and multiple consequences. The reform era preceding World War I had a profound effect on the national consciousness. Therefore, a number of factors must be investigated to understand what led to U.S. involvement in what was essentially a European conflict. A good many people, events, and issues should be placed into context.

Student pages

Focus on Research | *The United States in World War I and After*

Have students write down explanatory phrases for all of the topics in the seven rectangles on the activity sheet. Later, as a hands-on activity, they cut the sections and prepare a study booklet.

Hands-on Activity | *Preparing Study Booklets*

Give each student one sheet of colored paper to cut into fourths. The student cuts, folds, and staples the fourths as illustrated below to form an eight-page, fold-over booklet. The title and rectangles on the research sheet are cut out and glued in numerical order onto the pages of the booklet. The result is a study guide on the causes and consequences of World War I.

Students carefully fold the colored paper into fourths and then cut on the fold lines. The four pieces are arranged so that a small amount of each sheet shows below the sheet above. They fold over away from themselves so that each sheet shows below the one above it. The title and the seven topical rectangles are glued onto individual pages.

Fold-over Study Booklet

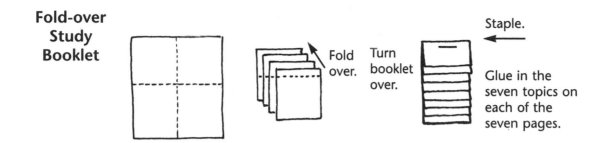

Fold over.

Turn booklet over.

Staple.

Glue in the seven topics on each of the seven pages.

Focus on Thinking *Missouri* vs. *Holland*

In order to understand the internationalism that was growing during the Progressive Era, students will consider the Supreme Court case of *Missouri* vs. *Holland*. They use the following format for analysis. Read Justice Holmes' decision to them after they have made their own decisions.

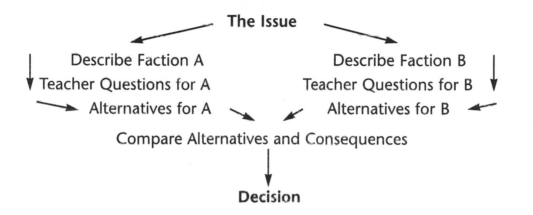

Justice Oliver Wendall Holmes wrote this decision for the court in 1920: "treaties made under the authority of the United States along with the Constitution and laws of the United States . . . are declared the supreme law of the land." As to the idea that the birds belong to the state, he said that the birds did not belong to the state because, "yesterday (they) had not arrived, tomorrow may be in another state, and in a week a thousand miles away . . . We see nothing in the Constitution that compels the government to sit by while a food supply is cut off and the protectors of our forests and of our crops destroyed."

Focus on Writing *Writing an Evidence Statement*

Students are asked to select and analyze a controversial statement by deciding to what extent they agree with it. After placing their judgment on a continuum from definitely false to definitely true, they write down words from the reading that influenced them. These words are then used to write a coherent opinion about the evidence supporting or refuting the statement. Some possible statements for analysis are listed on the sheet, but the teacher may want to suggest others.

What Do You Know About World War I?

Students signal answers to multiple-choice questions by using response cards marked with ABCD. They will also use the response cards to categorize events as happening prior to, during, or after World War I. The pattern for response cards is provided in "Make an Every Pupil Response Card" in the "Moving Toward Restructuring" section.

Focus on Sequence *Make a Time Line*

This section ends with a time line page. Directions for making a fan-fold time line booklet are given in "The Explorers Move Out" section.

The United States in World War I and After

Write a few explanatory words under each topic.
Cut out and glue into a fold-over study booklet.
Notice that all notes are written above the section names.

Lusitania

Zimmermann

Russian Revolution

1. Propaganda and Neutrality

Women

Blacks

Farmers

Businessmen

2. Impact on People

Airplanes and Dirigibles

Tanks

Trench Warfare

U-boats and Submarine Warfare

Poison Gas

3. Dueling Weapons

Wilson's 14 Points

Treaty of Versailles

Debate on and Signing of the Treaty

4. Ending the War

Manners and Morals

Religious Matters and the Law

Prohibition

Woman's Suffrage

Women in New Roles

Black Renaissance

5. Social Change

Archduke Ferdinand

Kaiser Wilhelm

Woodrow Wilson

Herbert Hoover

John Pershing

6. People to Remember

Nationalism and Rivalries

Wartime Powers

Nations Emerge and Change

Bonds and Debt

Isolationist Sentiment

Social Change

Prosperity and Depression

7. Causes and Consequences

Preparing Study Booklets

Make certain that you have written notes on each of the topics on the research page. Use those notes to glue into your study booklet.

Take one piece of colored paper and cut it into fourths. If you wish to make a larger booklet, use two pieces of paper cut in half. Arrange the four new pieces so that a small amount of each sheet shows below the sheet above.

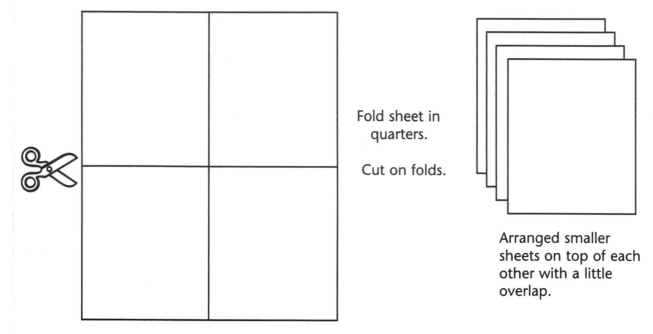

Fold sheet in quarters.

Cut on folds.

Arranged smaller sheets on top of each other with a little overlap.

Fold over the sheets turning away from you so that there are now eight overlapping sheets. Turn the booklet from back to front and staple at the top. You now have an eight-page fold-over booklet. Cut out the title and rectangles on the research sheet and glue them in numerical order at the bottom of the pages of the booklet so that the number and topic show.

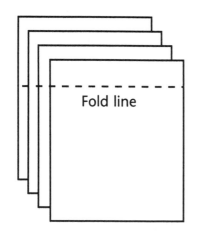

Fold line

Fold away from you.

Turn to front.

There will be eight overlapping sheets.

Staple and glue title on first sheet.

Glue rectangles with notes onto each of other seven pages.

Title	
1	
2	
3	
4	
5	
6	
7	

You now have a study guide on the causes and consequences of World War I. You can use it to study alone or in pairs.

Missouri vs. Holland

In the early 1900s, Congress passed a law that was aimed at controlling the shooting of migratory birds. District courts ruled that this was an unconstitutional use of federal power to regulate commerce. These lower court rulings held that the birds belonged to the states for the benefit of their residents and that the national government had no constitutional right to regulate them.

In order to get around this decision, the U.S. government signed a treaty with Great Britain that protected the migration of birds between the United States and Canada. The treaty said that there was a threat that these birds might become extinct. It set out protective measures such as closed seasons. It also said that each country agreed to pass laws that would protect the birds. Congress then passed the Migratory Bird Treaty Act of 1918. It set out federal regulations controlling the shooting of these birds. The state of Missouri filed a suit to try to prevent a federal game warden from enforcing the act.

1. Describe the government's point of view. _____ _____

   _____

2. Why was a treaty signed? _____ _____ _____

   _____

3. Explain the point of view of the state of Missouri. _____

   _____

4. Whose rights did they think were not being considered? _____

   _____

5. Compare the alternatives and consequences for the state and national governments.

   _____

   _____

6. Whose point of view do you think was supported by the Supreme Court? _____

   _____

7. How do you think the decision was backed up? _____

   _____

Name _____

Writing an Evidence Statement

Write a controversial statement about the Progressive Era.

_____
_____
_____

Make a judgment about your statement by placing a check in one circle.

◯	1	Definitely False
◯	2	Probably False
◯	3	Possibly False
◯	4	Uncertain
◯	5	Possibly True
◯	6	Probably True
◯	7	Definitely True

Write some words that influenced your selection.

_____
_____
_____
_____
_____
_____
_____

Justify your judgment selection by composing two or three evidence sentences explaining why you made this judgment.

_____
_____
_____
_____
_____
_____
_____
_____

Possible statements could be
"The way the United States obtained the Panama Canal Zone was justified by the results."
"We could solve city problems today just like they did in the Progressive Era."
"The muckrakers needed to exaggerate the problems they saw to get people's attention."
"The entry of the United States into World War I was inevitable."
"True American patriotism is always intolerant."

What Do You Know About World War I?

Use "Every Pupil Response Cards" to Signal Answers

1. The assassination of this man in Sarajevo was the focal point for the beginning of World War I. He was
   A. a kaiser.
   B. an archduke.
   C. a president.

2. The American president in 1914 was
   A. Wilson.
   B. Roosevelt.
   C. Wilhelm.

3. The new weapon called Big Bertha was
   A. a cannon.
   B. a long trench.
   C. a tube of chlorine gas.

4. Because the British had prevented most cargo from reaching Germany, the kaiser decided to use
   A. dirigibles.   B. U-Boats.
   C. tanks.   D. poison gas.

5. A telegram sent to Mexico which reached the United States was sent by
   A. Sussex.   B. Hughes.
   C. Lusitania.   D. Zimmermann.

6. One result of our involvement in World War I was the movement of
   A. women off the farms.
   B. blacks to northern factories.
   C. Russians to Brest-Litovsk.

7. Trench warfare meant that
   A. very few people were actually killed.
   B. poison gas was not dangerous.
   C. there were few pitched battles.

8. The man in charge of the Food Administration was
   A. Charles Evans Hughes.
   B. Herbert Hoover.
   C. John J. Pershing.

9. Black Jack Pershing got his nickname because he
   A. led an all-black unit at one time.
   B. had an extremely dark beard.
   C. always wore black boots.

Place these into three categories:
  A. A cause for U.S. involvement in World War I
  B. An event of World War I here or in Europe
  C. A consequence of World War I for Americans
Select and read randomly from different groups.

A

System of alliances
The sinking of the *Lusitania* off Ireland
Nations were competing for colonies
Propaganda to win the support of the United States
The Sussex pledge
The British blockade to prevent contraband
The Zimmermann telegram sent to Mexico

B

The Selective Service Act
George M. Cohan wrote "Over There"
Treaty of Brest-Litovsk
War Industry Board under Bernard Baruch
Tanks, airplanes, and dirigibles
General John J. Pershing landed in Europe
Planting Victory Gardens
Buying Liberty Bonds
Blacks left the South for better jobs
Soldiers blinded and killed by poison gas
The Espionage and Sedition Acts
Bolshevik Revolution in Russia
Defeating U-boats with the convoy system
Herbert Hoover organized food program
Wilson's 14 Points
Women assumed new roles

C

Isolationist fears grew in the U.S. Senate
New nations were formed
Senate refused to ratify Peace Treaty
United States failed to join League of Nations
The 1920s became a decade of great prosperity
The Harlem Renaissance
Nations were supposed to pay reparations
The United States moved into a time of social change
Women began to enjoy new careers
Freedoms, manners and morals changed
Aircraft developed for many purposes

Make a Time Line

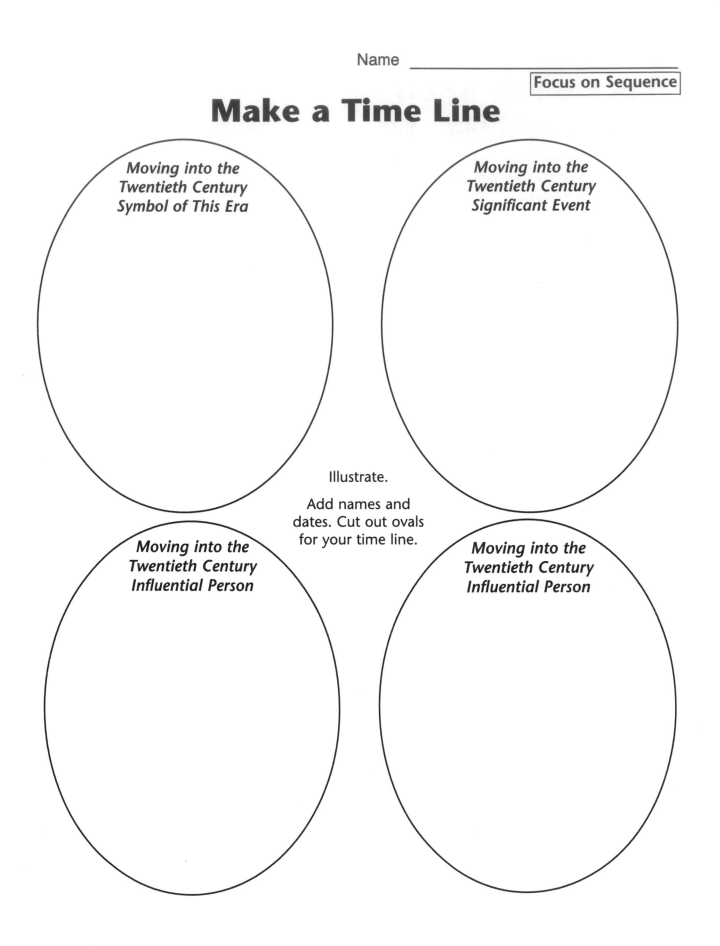

*Moving into the
Twentieth Century
Symbol of This Era*

*Moving into the
Twentieth Century
Significant Event*

Illustrate.

Add names and
dates. Cut out ovals
for your time line.

*Moving into the
Twentieth Century
Influential Person*

*Moving into the
Twentieth Century
Influential Person*

Movements of the 1920s and 1930s

After World War I came to an end, Americans were ready to look inward and concentrate on domestic affairs. Presidential candidate Warren Harding called it a "return to normalcy." Private concerns preoccupied most Americans until 1929, when the stock market crash made them turn to government for solutions to economic problems.

During most of the "Roaring Twenties," business activity reached an all-time high. Very few Americans were unemployed. But then the weakness in the economic system brought prosperity to a halt. Hundreds of businesses failed. People began to lose their jobs and then their homes, farms, and life savings.

By the time Franklin D. Roosevelt was elected president in 1932, the nation was in the midst of the Great Depression. His New Deal brought a three-way attack on the situation. First, Congress passed relief measures to provide for the millions of unemployed and needy. Then came efforts to revive agriculture and industry and bolster the economy. And finally, laws and regulations were designed to protect against future economic catastrophes.

Yet even as the economy rose and fell, innovative ideas and new technology were creating a new way of living. The automobile and hard-surfaced roads allowed people to move back and forth between country and city. Electric lights, airplanes, radio, and motion pictures all added to the new national culture. Alongside the new technology came a surge of interest in the arts, represented by the originality and fresh approach of the Harlem Renaissance. This neighborhood in New York City became a gathering place for black poets, writers, performers, painters, and musicians. The emotional richness of their work influenced black and white Americans alike.

But nationalism and power politics in Europe and Asia soon forced the country to become involved in the affairs of other countries again.

Just for Teachers

Background Information:

A desire to keep the stability of older ways dominated a great many social values at this time. The Immigration Law of 1924 established a quota system that discriminated against all groups except northern and western Europeans. The Ku Klux Klan attacked blacks, Roman Catholics, and Jews. And in 1925, in Dayton, Tennessee, a high school science teacher was convicted of teaching Darwinian theories of evolution, which fundamentalist Protestants bitterly opposed. Many people were even suspicious of the modern technology that was quickly creating a higher standard of living.

Then, just as people were adjusting to having all kinds of new products and more time for education and recreation, the Great Depression struck. For several frightening years, life for many Americans became a grim struggle for survival. When the whole world was plunged into economic turmoil, Americans turned inward. The American people were not interested in world leadership, and they were determined to stay out of war.

It took the specter of the dictators of Japan, Italy, and Germany crushing their weaker neighbors for Americans to recognize the danger. In place of the faith and good will at the end of the war, the world was filled with international rivalries, suspicions, and distrust. As the armies of Japan, Italy, and Germany began to march into weaker countries, neutrality was abandoned. American farms and factories began to produce food and war materials to be shipped to Europe.

The cost of the war was enormous both in human lives and in capital resources. Farms and factories and whole sections of major cities were destroyed. Around eight million military personnel were killed and many more millions of civilian deaths resulted from bombings, starvation, disease, and imprisonment.

Student pages

| Focus on Research | *The Arts Live On*

Students research the writers, painters, musicians, and poets of the Harlem Renaissance and information about what they did and write it on the activity sheet. Expect names like Langston Hughes, W. E. B. DuBois, W. C. Handy, Louis Armstrong, Duke Ellington, Marian Anderson, Countee Cullen, Jean Toomer, Richard Wright, Alain Locke, Claude McKay, Rudolph Fisher, John and James Johnson, and Carl Van Vechtor.

Categorizing Two Decades

Students assist each other in categorizing different events during the Roaring Twenties and the Great Depression as contained in specialized folders. Cut out pictures and short articles and glue into colored folders, using titles such as these: Women in the Depression, Hard Times, Stock Market Crash, Artists of the 1930s, Prohibition, Prosperity, Industrial Growth and Prosperity, The Golden Twenties, Entertainers and Writers, Harlem Renaissance, and Technological Changes. On each folder, glue a 1920s and 1930s data retrieval chart. Similar charts are to be constructed by students on poster board using the sample on the folders as a guide. Pass folders from group to group so that students can record information on their charts with markers. Share charts.

Focus on Skills | *Where Did the Events Happen?*

Have students make a list of significant events during the years 1930 to 1945. Each event is to be coded using the number assigned to the part of the world in which it happened. After the lists are complete, students take turns reading from their lists while the other members of the groups signal the location by holding up the correct number of fingers. One finger is for the United States, two for Great Britain, three for Europe, and four for Africa or Asia. This activity allows all students to answer at once without making noise.

Focus on Review | *Catch a Question*

The question catcher is a form of a folded paper game played by children the world over. In this case, it is turned into a device with which one of these pairs of students can ask each other questions about the topic. After playing with Roaring Twenties devices distributed by the teacher, students are to make their own question catchers with their own review questions. Although making the question catchers should be an individual effort, it would be wise to divide the material so that all parts of the topic will be covered. Assigning each row or table a separate part of the textbook chapter is one way to accomplish this goal.

Focus on Thinking | *United States vs. Curtiss Wright Export Corp*

A desire to keep from being dragged into the troubles of other nations does not mean that there will not be controversy, particularly when business interests are involved. Students analyze this case that arose when the president declared an embargo in the name of national security. Afterwards, they can hear the court decision.

Justice Sutherland wrote the opinion following the 7-1 vote. He said that the national government could take action in conducting foreign affairs that might exceed its authority to direct domestic policy. Some powers were not listed in the Constitution because the United States was a sovereign nation and was so before the Constitution was written. (Congress) "must often accord to the president a degree of discretion and freedom from statutory restriction which would not be admissible were domestic affairs alone involved."

Focus on Maps | *Allied and Axis Powers During World War II*

On a map of Europe, students mark who was in control of Europe at the peak of Germany's power in 1942. They are asked to color-code the map to show which countries were Allies, Axis, Axis-controlled, or neutral.

Focus on Writing | *Hoover and Roosevelt*

After adjusting the illustration, students seek out phrases that describe the two men and write the phrases in the boxes. Then, have students write a compare-and-contrast paragraph.

Hands-on Activity | *Tree of Life in the Great Depression*

Students write events and situations during the Great Depression on the leaves on the activity sheet. The leaves are glued onto a large tree that students have drawn on poster board and cut out. Students include phrases such as bonus army, soup kitchens, married women barred from teaching, Boulder Dam built, Brain Trust's ideas for Roosevelt, Twentieth Amendment.

Focus on Sequence | *Make a Time Line*

This section ends with a time line page. Directions for making a fan-fold time line booklet are given in "The Explorers Move Out" section.

The Arts Live On

These silhouettes represent people who were active in the Harlem Renaissance. Write a name and accomplishment beside each figure. You may want to add a little color to your sheet.

Categorizing Two Decades

	The Roaring Twenties 1920s	The Great Depression 1930s
Business		
Daily Life		
Literature Music Art		
Workers		
Politics		
Social Issues		
Famous People		

Where Did the Events Happen?

Glue this on the front of a 5" x 8" card.

1	UNITED STATES
2	GREAT BRITAIN
3	EUROPEAN CONTINENT
4	AFRICA AND ASIA

Glue these on the back of the card. Add at least ten events of your own. Take turns reading them aloud to the other members of your group. They will answer by holding up the correct number of fingers. When everyone has signaled, point to the correct answer.

Roosevelt begins the New Deal (1)
The dust bowl caused migration (1)
John Dillinger and J. Edgar Hoover (1)
Mahatma Gandhi leads the salt march (4)
Japan invades Manchuria (4)
Winston Churchill leads the nation (2)
UAW and the GM Sit-Down Strike (1)
Rommel wins at El Alamein (4)

Edward VIII gives up the throne (2)
Benito Mussolini rose to power (3)
The Scottsboro case (1)
The Blitzkrieg begins (2)
Chamberlain resigns (2)
Siege of Leningrad and Stalingrad (3)
Zeppelin made airships popular(3)

_____
_____
_____
_____

Catch a Question

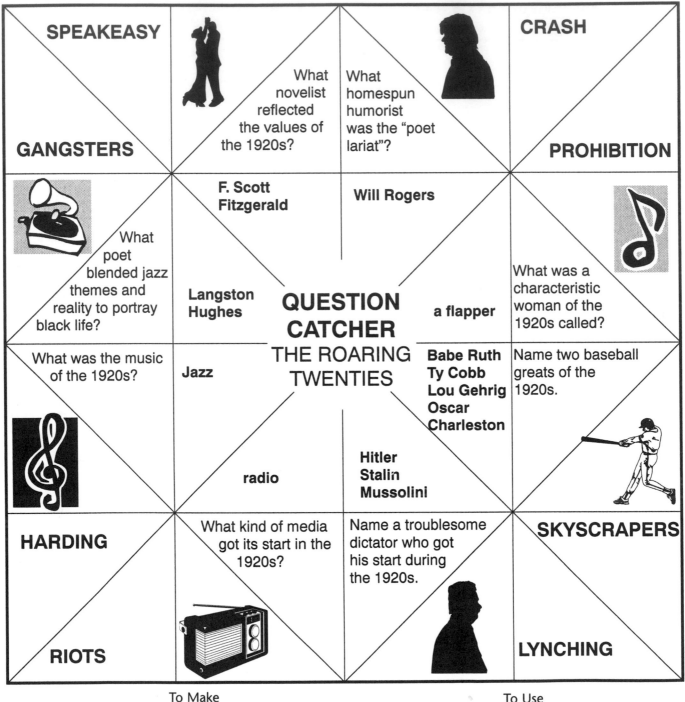

SPEAKEASY

What novelist reflected the values of the 1920s?

What homespun humorist was the "poet lariat"?

CRASH

GANGSTERS

PROHIBITION

F. Scott Fitzgerald

Will Rogers

What poet blended jazz themes and reality to portray black life?

Langston Hughes

QUESTION CATCHER
THE ROARING TWENTIES

a flapper

What was a characteristic woman of the 1920s called?

What was the music of the 1920s?

Jazz

Babe Ruth
Ty Cobb
Lou Gehrig
Oscar Charleston

Name two baseball greats of the 1920s.

Hitler
Stalin
Mussolini

radio

HARDING

What kind of media got its start in the 1920s?

Name a troublesome dictator who got his start during the 1920s.

SKYSCRAPERS

RIOTS

LYNCHING

To Make

1. Cut out the square.
2. Turn it face down on the desk.
3. Fold each corner to the center.
4. Turn the four triangles face down.
5. Again, fold each corner to the center.
6. Place thumbs and forefingers under the flaps.

To Use

1. Ask a friend to choose a word.
2. Spell out the word reversing directions.
3. Ask your friend to pick out a symbol.
4. Lift the symbol and ask the question.
5. The right answer is under the question.

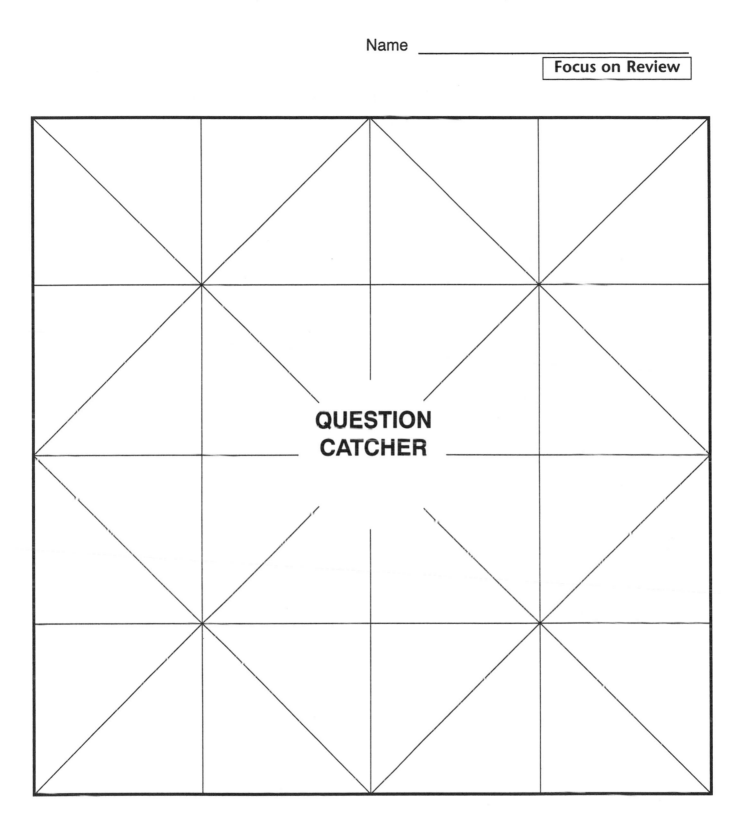

**QUESTION
CATCHER**

Make your own review question catcher. Fold a plain piece of paper, following the directions on the question catcher already constructed. The fold lines make the divisions as shown above. Name your question catcher according to the topic you are studying. Make up eight questions and write them where indicated. Now write the answer to each question. Add eight words that are important to remember. Put in numbers or draw pictures for identification. Play the review game with a friend.

United States vs. Curtiss Wright Export Corp

You are going to consider the case of *United States* vs. *Curtiss-Wright Export Corporation*, which came before the Supreme Court in 1936. European nations were just three years away from war. Americans did not want to be dragged into their troubles. In this case, the broad powers of the president in matters of national security are being questioned. The effect of Supreme Court interpretations in international relations is illustrated. Use this plan to reach your own conclusions before your teacher tells you what the court decided.

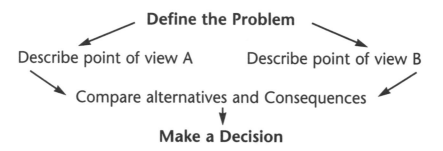

On May 28, 1934, President Franklin Roosevelt issued an embargo on the sale of any arms and munitions to Paraguay or Bolivia by U.S. companies. He was acting under the power granted to him by a joint resolution of Congress. The two countries were at war with each other and the United States did not want to be in any way involved in the conflict. Curtiss Wright went ahead and sold machine guns to Bolivia. The federal government brought them to court for violating the embargo. Curtiss Wright claimed that Congress did not have the right to empower the president to issue such a ruling. They said it was an unlawful delegation of legislative power. The company felt that Congress was letting the president make laws. Since the Constitution gave that power to Congress, it would make the embargo invalid.

What is the problem? _____

_____

Why did Curtiss Wright say the embargo was unconstitutional?	Why did the president feel he had the right to issue an embargo?

What do you think was decided? _____

_____

Allied and Axis Powers During World War II

On this map of Europe, show who was in control of Europe at the peak of the Axis power in 1942. Color code your map to show which countries were Allies, which were Axis nations, which were controlled by the Axis nations, and which were neutral.

Hoover and Roosevelt

At the 1933 inauguration, Herbert Hoover and Franklin Roosevelt rode in the same car. Write descriptive words in the boxes below. Use these descriptive words to help you write a compare-and-contrast-paragraph.

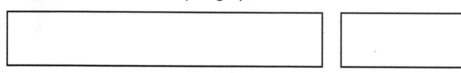

Tree of Life in the Great Depression

Draw a big tree on a large sheet of construction paper or on poster board. Label it "Tree of Life in the Great Depression." Cut it out. On the leaves below, write about things that happened to people at this time. Also write about events that took place. Cut out your leaves and glue them to the tree.

When you need more leaves, just trace one that you have already cut out.

Make a Time Line

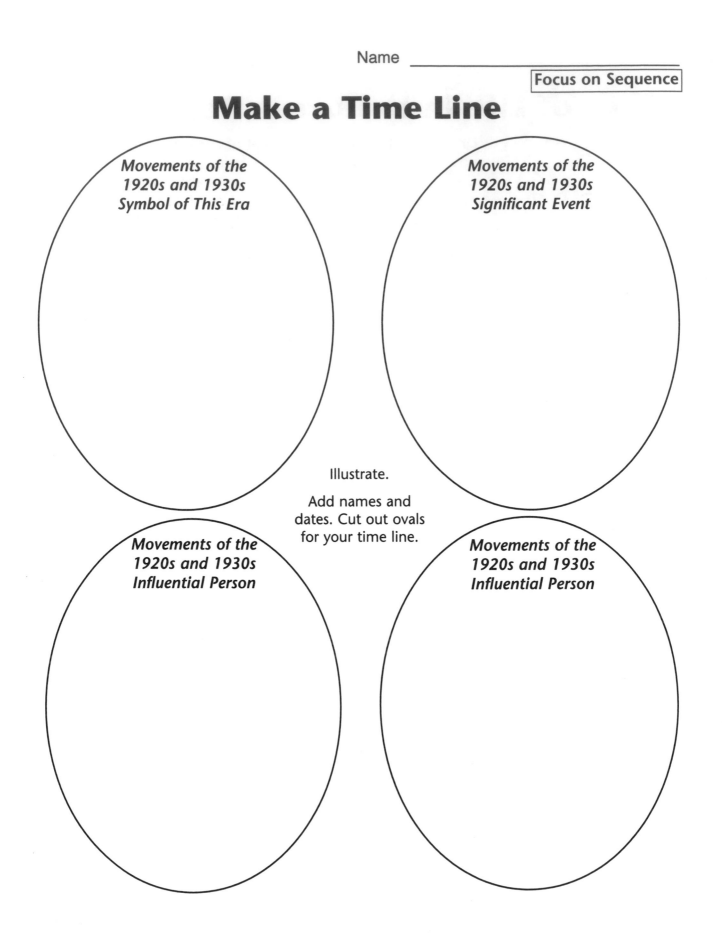

Movements of the
1920s and 1930s
Symbol of This Era

Movements of the
1920s and 1930s
Significant Event

Illustrate.

Add names and
dates. Cut out ovals
for your time line.

Movements of the
1920s and 1930s
Influential Person

Movements of the
1920s and 1930s
Influential Person

Moving into a Cold War

Between 1945 and the early 1960s, there were plenty of jobs to go around. The United States was producing a fascinating variety of goods for people who had done without during wartime shortages. Government-backed loans made it possible for young married couples to buy new homes for a down payment of only a few hundred dollars. Cars with exciting new designs rolled off the assembly lines and into the family garage. America's factories were making all kinds of labor-saving devices for homes and farms. Medical science produced thousands of new medical products such as the anti-polio vaccine. Never before in history had so many people enjoyed so much prosperity. People were too busy concentrating on getting ahead to care about world affairs.

During the postwar years, the United States government sought to remove the threat of war and to strengthen peaceful democratic governments. The Marshall Plan was put into place to help the war-torn countries of Europe rebuild. Aid was provided for the emerging nations in the less-developed parts of the world. At the same time, the United States developed a foreign policy that sought to stop the spread of communism. Military aid was offered to friendly and nonaligned nations. Collective defense arrangements, such as NATO and SEATO, were formed.

The cold war first began because the U.S.S.R. used military force to install communist governments in Eastern Europe. These Soviet actions were in opposition to the U.S. government's insistence upon the right of all people to determine the kind of government they wanted. It raised fears that the U.S.S.R., after gaining control of Eastern Europe, would try to communize Western Europe. On the other hand, the Russians had suffered enormous losses in the war against Nazi Germany and felt that control of Eastern Europe would prevent another invasion from Western Europe. The Soviets believed there had been a wartime understanding that created spheres of influence in Europe. Soon Eastern Europe was separated from Western nations by a military and political barrier often called the Iron Curtain.

Just for Teachers

Political differences between the United States and the Soviet Union were aggravated by ideological conflict. American public opinion focused on the idea that normal relations with any communist government were impossible. The U.S. strategy was one of containment or resistance to the spread of Russian influence. This policy appeared to the U.S.S.R. as one more Western effort to isolate and undermine the Soviet system. The Marxist-Leninist Soviet leaders believed that capitalism would inevitably seek the destruction of the Soviet system. In the United States, a long-standing suspicion and dislike of communism strengthened the view that the U.S.S.R. was intent on expansion and world conquest.

This cold war continued until the early years of the Reagan administration. However, when Mikhail Gorbachev came to power in 1985, the situation began to change dramatically. Gorbachev's policy of reconciliation with the West led to quasi-democratic governments for the satellite countries of Eastern Europe. And the symbolic Berlin Wall came tumbling down.

Student pages

Focus on Research *People Who Influenced the Postwar World*

Students research one person that fits the category in each of the quadrants in the circle on the activity sheet. Afterwards, they are to write a short description of how that person had an impact on people's lives in the years after World War II.

People they might choose to research include Linda Brown, Chiang Kai-shek, Winston Churchill, Dick Clark, Thomas Dewey, Dwight D. Eisenhower, John Kennedy, Martin Luther King, Jr., Nikita Khrushchev, William Levitt, Douglas MacArthur, Joseph McCarthy, Mao Zedong (also spelled Tse-tung), George Marshall, Thurgood Marshall, Richard Nixon, Rosa Parks, Jackson Pollock, Elvis Presley, Jackie Robinson, J. D. Salinger, Jonas Salk, Joseph Stalin, Ed Sullivan, Robert Taft, Harry Truman, Earl Warren

Politician / Entertainer / Innovator / Leader

Hands-on Activity *Each One Teach*

Students cut up the rectangles on the activity sheet and randomly divide them among members of the group. Groups have ten minutes for each person to share what is on his or her cards. Encourage students to tell something else they know about the event to aid group members in remembering the information. When time is called, all cards are to be placed face down in a pile. Then, the teacher asks students to list all of the facts they can remember on the time line.

Focus on Skills | *Time Line of Critical Events from 1945 to 1960*

Make a transparency of the time line and have the class record the 12 bits of information that they remember from "Each One Teach." Afterwards, distribute copies of the time line for students to record both this information and other pieces of information from this era that they feel are important.

Focus on Interpretation | *It Happened in the Fifties*

Students role-play scenes from the 1950s. Cut up the slips of paper and hand them out to teams of students. Each team has its members assume roles and act out the situation. Debrief students afterward to see what they learned from acting out these events.

Focus on Writing | *Contrasting the United States After WWI and WWII*

A Pulitzer Prize-winning historian, Daniel Boorstin, says that after World War II there was a "dramatic departure from earlier American policy: a leap from the war-debt psychology of foreign aid, from the vocabulary of the banker to that of the missionary, the humanitarian and the social scientist. After World War I, politicians had talked of reparation and 'honest debtors,' of interest rates, and the capacity of countries to pay back what they had borrowed. Now after World War II, they were talking about standards of living."

After listening to this quote, students are to consider other areas where there was a dramatic change of attitude from after World War I to after World War II. They are to write these contrasts In the rectangles on the activity sheet. After discussing the charts in class and adding to their activity sheets, students will construct a short compare-and-contrast essay.

Focus on Sequence | *Make a Time Line*

This section ends with a time line page. Directions for making a fan-fold time line booklet are given in "The Explorers Move Out" section.

People Who Influenced the Postwar World

Choose one person to research for each of the four categories in the circle. Be certain you can explain how the person you have chosen will fit the category. In each section of the circle, write a short description of how the people you selected had an impact on people's lives in the years following World War II.

People you might choose to research include Linda Brown, Chiang Kai-shek, Winston Churchill, Dick Clark, Thomas Dewey, Dwight D. Eisenhower, John Kennedy, Martin Luther King, Jr., Nikita Khrushchev, William Levitt, Douglas MacArthur, Joseph McCarthy, Mao Zedong (also spelled Tse-tung), George Marshall, Thurgood Marshall, Richard Nixon, Rosa Parks, Jackson Pollock, Elvis Presley, Jackie Robinson, J. D. Salinger, Jonas Salk, Joseph Stalin, Ed Sullivan, Robert Taft, Harry Truman, Earl Warren

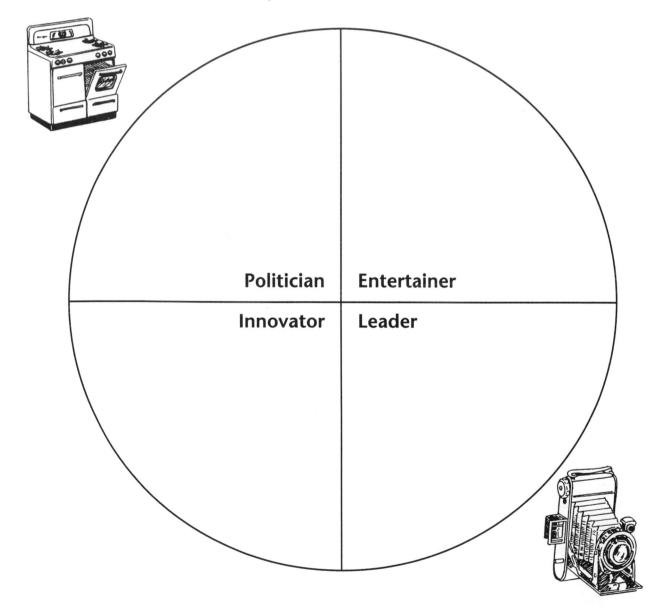

Politician Entertainer

Innovator Leader

Each One Teach

Cut up the rectangles on this activity sheet and randomly divide them among the members of your group. You will then have ten minutes for each person to share what is on his or her cards. When time is called, place cards face down in a pile. You will then be asked to list all of the facts you can remember on a time line.

In 1954, the Supreme Court outlawed "separate but equal" schools in *Brown* vs. *Board of Education*.	In 1945, Roosevelt died, and Harry Truman became president. Truman took part in the Yalta conference.	In 1948, the Russians banned all traffic between the western zone and Berlin. The resulting airlift flew in 4,000 tons of supplies each day.
In 1955, Rosa Parks refused to move to the back of the bus and began the Montgomery bus boycott.	In 1945, the United States dropped an atomic bomb on Hiroshima, which brought an end to the war in Asia. VE-Day soon followed.	In 1949, the Communists took over China, and the Nationalist government moved to Taiwan.
In 1956, under President Eisenhower, the Federal Highway Act started the building of an interstate highway system.	In 1947, the Truman Doctrine to support freedom around the world was declared. The Marshall Plan to rebuild Europe was a direct result.	In 1957, the Russians launched *Sputnik*, the first unmanned artificial satellite to orbit the earth; the race for space began.
In 1958, the National Defense Education Act (NDEA) began funding special equipment for schools.	In 1948, Jewish residents of Palestine proclaimed an independent Israel. The United Nations recognized this new nation.	In 1954, the French were defeated in Indochina. Vietnam was divided in half. SEATO was formed to protect noncommunist nations.

Time Line of Critical Events
From 1945 to 1960

1945 _____
_____
1946 _____
_____
1947 _____
_____
1948 _____
_____
1949 _____
_____
1950 _____
_____
1951 _____
_____
1952 _____
_____
1953 _____
_____
1954 _____
_____
1955 _____
_____
1956 _____
_____
1957 _____
_____
1958 _____
_____
1959 _____
_____
1960 _____
_____

It Happened in the Fifties

Harry Truman is reading the newspaper headlines based on early returns that said Dewey had won the 1948 election. Someone announces that, based on later returns from the farm belt, Truman had won by over 100 electoral votes.

Senator Joseph McCarthy and the Un-American Activities Committee is conducting a hearing in Washington. Several well-known Hollywood personalities testify about their affiliation with groups that might be considered communist front organizations.

At the 1952 Republican convention, Dwight Eisenhower is selected as the nominee and Richard Nixon is then named as his running mate. Many delegates are waving "I Like Ike" signs.

Paratroopers stand outside Little Rock High School to ensure that the integration will be peaceful. Black students walk between the paratroopers as racist citizens stand and jeer and predict violence.

A family has just bought a new television set. The little kids talk about seeing Howdy Doody, the teenagers about hearing Dick Clark's *American Bandstand,* and the parents about watching Ed Sullivan and Milton Berle.

Vice President Nixon of the United States and the Soviet Union's Nikita Khrushchev hold a "kitchen debate" at a model American kitchen on display in Moscow in 1959.

President Eisenhower visits with troops in Korea to ask them how the war is going and what they think about the peace talks.

Name _____

Contrasting the United States After WWI and WWII

Consider the focus of each concern below where there was a dramatic change of attitude from after World War I to after World War II. Write these contrasts in the rectangles below the question. You will then use this activity sheet to construct a short compare-and-contrast essay.

How did Congress and the rest of the country prepare for returning veterans?

After World War I	After World War II

What was the United States' attitude toward European nations?

After World War I	After World War II

What was the relationship between labor unions and the changing economy?

After World War I	After World War II

What changes happened in terms of population growth and shifts?

After World War I	After World War II

What was the attitude of the American public toward foreign relations?

After World War I	After World War II

What attitudes and situations prevailed in the area of race relations?

After World War I	After World War II

Make a Time Line

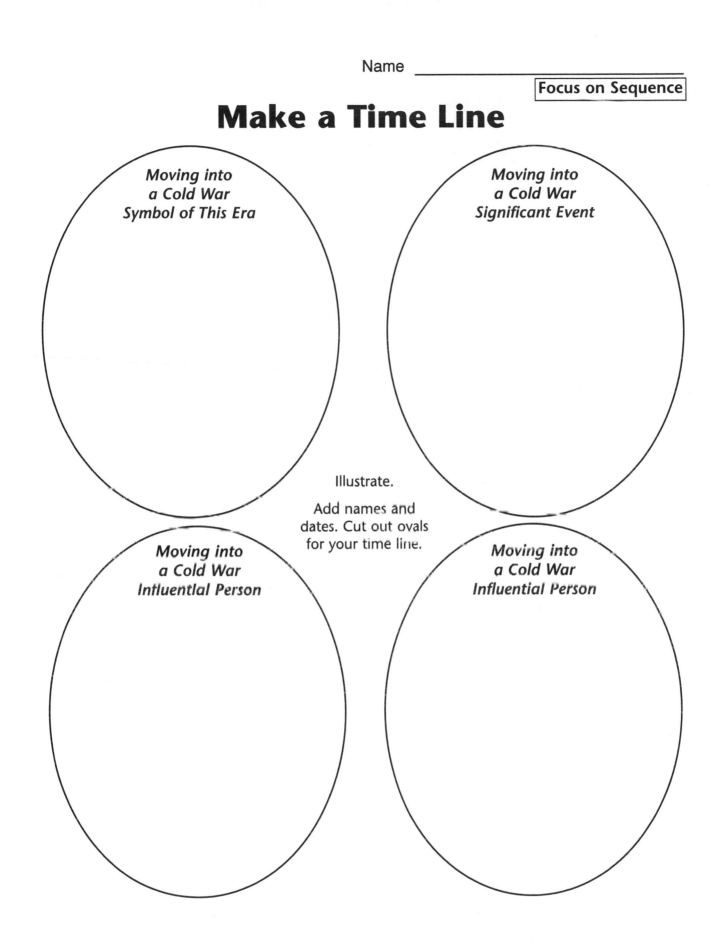

*Moving into
a Cold War
Symbol of This Era*

*Moving into
a Cold War
Significant Event*

Illustrate.

Add names and
dates. Cut out ovals
for your time line.

*Moving into
a Cold War
Influential Person*

*Moving into
a Cold War
Influential Person*

Moving Through Protest

The sixties and early seventies were disturbing and disorderly times in the United States. It was a period of both great idealism and great upheaval. One president was assassinated, another declined to run again because of opposition to an undeclared war, and a third, facing impeachment, resigned.

The era began when a new president with his beautiful wife and appealing children moved into the White House. The 45-year-old John F. Kennedy was a symbol of the optimism and idealism of the younger generation. But it lasted only 1,000 days. JFK survived the Bay of Pigs invasion of Cuba and the Cuban Missile Crisis to begin sending Peace Corps volunteers to underdeveloped countries and American military "advisors" into Vietnam. And then he was killed.

Civil Rights was already an issue when Kennedy took office, and it continued through the presidencies of Johnson and Nixon. In 1961, "freedom riders" took buses south to protest segregation of the races in bus stations. They were greeted by riots and beatings. In 1963, Martin Luther King, Jr.'s, drive to end segregation in Birmingham, Alabama, was met with cattle prods, snarling dogs, and fire hoses. And all of this was seen on television in the living rooms of the nation.

Frustration and resentment grew in the African-American sections of cities in the North and West. In 1965, the Watts area of Los Angeles erupted into a riot that lasted for several days and cost 34 people their lives. During the following three summers, outbursts of rebellion happened in cities across the country. The worst was the Detroit riot of 1967, which left 40 people dead and $250 million worth of property destroyed.

Another reason for protest was also filling the TV screens. The undeclared war in southeast Asia had become a killing field that gave rise to more and more unrest. University students held sit-ins and demonstrations, eventually causing President Johnson to decide not to run for another term.

It seemed that protest had become a national pastime. Ralph Nader protested the lack of safety in automobiles as Rachel Carson protested that pesticides were destroying wildlife. Cesar Chavez led a boycott of California grapes to protest the way Hispanic farm workers were treated, while Betty Friedan began the revolt of women against unequal opportunity in the workplace and in public life. And the hippies left home to become flower children of the counterculture.

Finally, the passions and upheavals of the 1960s gave way to at least the appearance of calm in the later 1970s and 1980s. Protests became less frequent as blacks and whites alike took stock of the gains of one of the most turbulent periods in U.S. history.

Just for Teachers

Thousands of boycotts, demonstrations, sit-ins, and marches occurred during this period as various advocates came on the scene and began to exert influence. Even though the demonstrators were usually well-disciplined and nonviolent, they often met bitter opposition. Reports and photographs of demonstrators being beaten or carried off by law enforcement officers had a strong impact on national opinion. The shooting of students at Kent State shocked everyone. The courts and the federal government began to respond to a growing popular indignation.

Each of these advocates had his or her particular message and means of delivery. Just as Martin Luther King, Jr., became the symbol of Civil Rights agitation, Ralph Nader emerged as the defender of American consumers against defective and unsafe products. Bob Dylan, with his folk protest songs like "Blowin' in the Wind," expressed the hopes and angers of his generation. And women like Gloria Steinem and Shirley Chisholm held up the hope for equal opportunity to women encouraged by feminist studies and a climate favorable to antidiscrimination movements.

For most Americans, the Vietnam War was different from previous wars. Peace advocates known as doves viewed it as immoral and an improper use of human and economic resources. Supporters or hawks believed the war necessary as a way to stop the spread of communism in Asia. When our troops were forced to return home without victory, many soldiers had difficulty adjusting to civilian life. It was not until 1982 that a memorial, designed by 21-year-old architecture student Maya Ying Lin, was erected in Washington, D.C., to honor Vietnam veterans.

Student pages

| Focus on Research | *Clipboard for Collecting Information on People Who Held Protests*

On the clipboard activity sheet, students record information about people of the protest era. They are to select one person for each of the four topics on the clipboard.

They might consider but should not be limited to these: Bella Abzug, Stokely Carmichael, Rachel Carson, Cesar Chavez, Bob Dylan, Medgar Evers, Betty Friedan, Jesse Jackson, Robert Kennedy, Martin Luther King, Jr., James Meredith, Ralph Nader, John and Mary Beth Tinker, and Malcolm X.

Focus on Writing — *Writing "But Now I Know" Poetry*

Students analyze what they learned about this period in history by writing a special kind of poem. The first line starts with "I used to think . . . ." This is followed by a second line that begins "But now I know . . . .". A sample of such a poem on another subject is given on the activity sheet. Ask them to consider all of the facts that have already been covered, but suggestions of topics are also included to jog the students' memories. Encourage them to guess what they might have said the word meant before you started the unit. Examples:

I used to think the March on Washington happened during the Revolutionary War
But now I know it was all about civil rights and Martin Luther King, Jr.'s, dream.
I used to think Rachel Carson was a teacher down the hall
But now I know she wrote a book about not hearing the birds anymore.

Hands-on Activity — *Protest Pyramid*

Students organize information regarding one of the protest movements of the 1960s and 1970s onto a pyramid. When the activity sheet is duplicated, it should be enlarged about 20 percent. On the four triangular sides of the pyramid, students place words and illustrations to show:

1. One person who was involved in this movement and what he/she did.
2. One nonviolent event of this protest that showed people's dedication.
3. One event of this protest that focused public opinion on the issues.
4. The positive results of this protest that can be seen today.

Afterwards they cut out the shape, fold on the lines, and glue the pyramid together.

Focus on Integration — *Constructing a Center*

The center illustrated on this activity page is one that could be constructed by the teacher or set up by a group of students as a special project. It is based on a thoughtful children's book, *The Wall*, by Eve Bunting, who also did an excellent book on Watts.

Focus on Sequence — *Make a Time Line*

This section ends with a time line page. Directions for making a fan-fold time line booklet are given in "The Explorers Move Out" section. Guide students in completing this project.

On this clipboard record information about four different people and the protests they led.

Clipboard for Collecting Information on People Who Led Protests

I protested a denial of Civil Rights	I protested the Vietnam War

I protested for unions and safety	I protested for equal opportunity

Writing "But Now I Know" Poetry

This sample poem on another subject is an example.

I used to think that cats would catch their own food.
But now I know that they expect to be fed if they live in my house.
I used to think camels be would neat to ride to school.
But now I know that they will spit right in your face.
I used to think that a skunk would make a nice pet.
But now I know I wouldn't want that smell in the house—ever.

You might consider what you have learned about freedom riders, integrating schools, riots, assassinations, marching through Selma, voter registration, Jim Crow, Nobel Peace Prize, separate but equal, Montgomery buses boycott, sit-ins, the grape boycott, the Equal Rights Amendment, spraying pesticides, Kent state, war on TV.

_____

I used to think _____
_____

But now I know _____
_____

I used to think _____
_____

But now I know _____
_____

I used to think _____
_____

But now I know _____
_____

I used to think _____
_____

But now I know _____
_____

Protest Pyramid

Organize information regarding one of the protest movements of the 1960s and 1970s onto this pyramid. Write your name and the type of protest movement on the square base. On the four triangular faces of the pyramid, put words and illustrations to show:

1. One person who was involved in this movement and what he/she did.
2. One nonviolent event of this movement that showed someone's dedication.
3. One event of this protest that focused public opinion on the issues.
4. The positive results of this protest that can be seen today.

Afterwards, cut out the shape, fold on the lines, and glue the pyramid together.

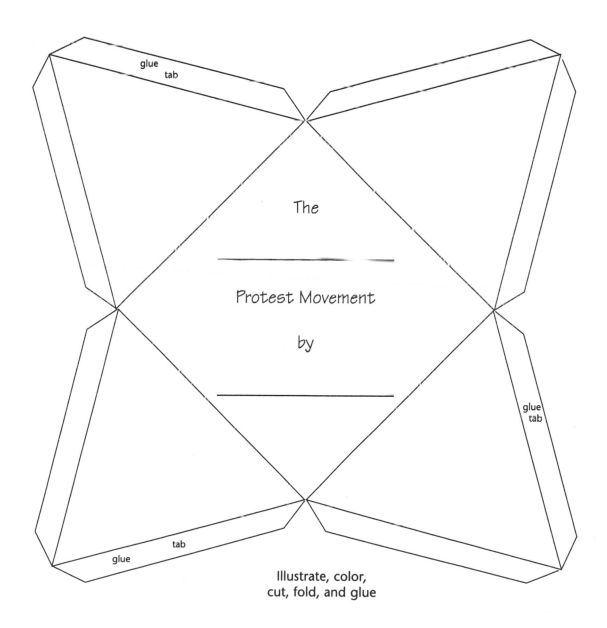

The

_____

Protest Movement

by

_____

glue tab

glue tab

glue tab

Illustrate, color,
cut, fold, and glue

Constructing a Center

Prepare a center such as the one sketched below. It is based on the book *The Wall* by Eve Bunting. Three sides of a large box that held a television or refrigerator can be covered with material, paper, or paint.

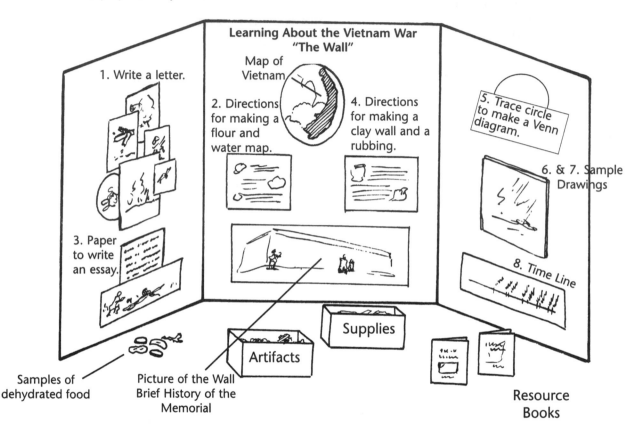

1. Assume you have a family member fighting in the war. Write to that person about things that are happening at home. Ask questions about what happens to a country when there is a war going on.
2. Make a flour-and-water map showing the landforms of Vietnam. After it is dry, use markers to make a key.
3. Write an essay about political events that led to the Vietnam War. Explain the United States' involvement.
4. Make a clay model of the Vietnam Veterans' memorial (The Wall). Put on names of people in this class. When it is dry, try making a rubbing.
5. Draw a Venn diagram of the points of view of the Viet Cong, the South Vietnamese, and the U.S. soldiers.
6. Make a drawing showing some of the equipment used during the war. Tell what each piece of equipment was used for.
7. Make a drawing of something you would bring if you should visit The Wall in Washington, D.C. Tell why you selected this object to place at the foot of The Wall to honor the soldiers.
8. Make a time line of the events of this time period.

Name _____

Make a Time Line

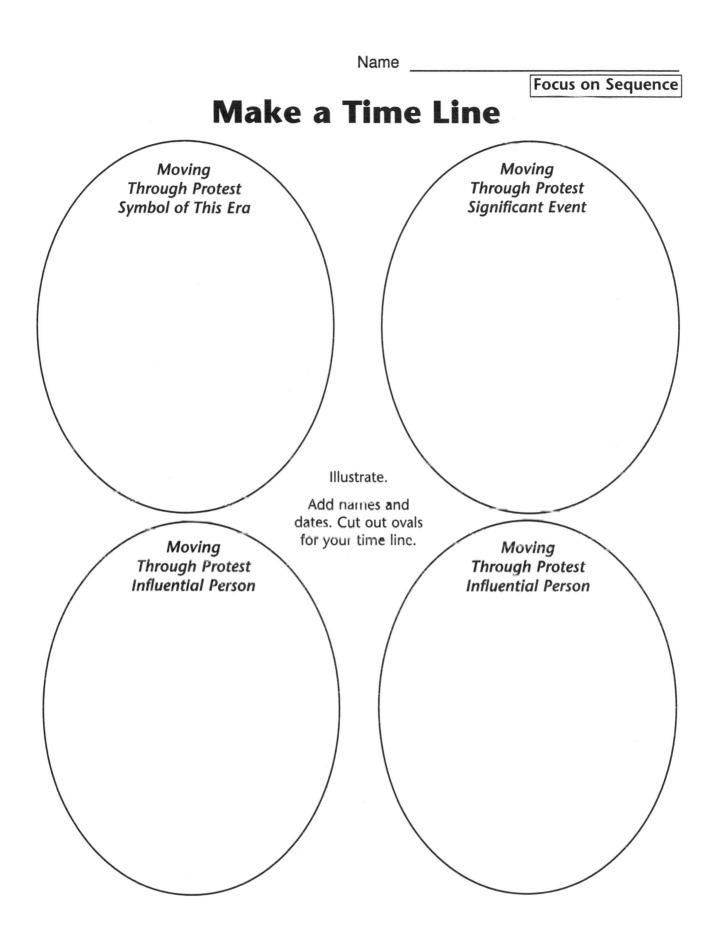

*Moving
Through Protest
Symbol of This Era*

*Moving
Through Protest
Significant Event*

Illustrate.

Add names and
dates. Cut out ovals
for your time line.

*Moving
Through Protest
Influential Person*

*Moving
Through Protest
Influential Person*

Moving Toward the Future

When people first moved to this continent, they had no idea what the future would hold. For them, our history lessons could only have been vague predictions.

It was a wonderful idea for that little band of pilgrims to venture across a frightening ocean. It was also right for a handful of colonies to challenge the power of Great Britain and strike out on their own. And all of the compromises on slavery would prove in the end to be useless. Finally, we agree that there are better ways to solve conflicts than to go to war.

When the signers of the Declaration of Independence met in Philadelphia in 1776, they had no idea that their small confederation would in two centuries become the world's greatest democracy. It is doubtful in their wildest expectations, they envisioned a nation of 300 million people, the strongest nation on earth.

From your study of *Movements in American History*, you should have learned that the future is always full of surprises. Now is the time to look backward and forward at the same time. What have we as a nation learned that will help us meet the mysterious promise of the future?

Just for Teachers

"If you do not learn about the mistakes of the past you are doomed to repeat them." This is the reason many teachers give students for studying history. But looking backward and finding historical precedents is dependent on remembering past events and placing them into context. At the conclusion of a year of studying American history, it might be a good idea to have students consider some of the issues with which we are now confronted to see if they can find any historical precedents. This may help them see implications for their own future.

Student pages

| Focus on Research | *Using the Newspaper*

Assign students to bring newspaper and news magazine articles that cover some of today's issues that have implications for the future. Challenge students to decide whether an article is one that has serious implications for their own future. The questions on the activity page are designed to lead students to consider how lessons from the past may assist us in determining the future.

The news articles should be shared with the class, for they will be the basis for the skills and hands-on activity sheets. You may wish to consider the number of groups you will use and assign topics for the articles accordingly. Possible topics include homelessness, urban violence, chemical abuse, child abuse, social security, gun control, education, illegal immigration, etc.

| Focus on Skills | *Collecting and Using Statistical Data*

Ask the whole class to think about the issues that concern people today as they think about the future. Have them decide the six issues they want to consider. Each student is to write them in the same order on his/her paper. Afterwards, they decide how to rate each of the issues from not very important to extremely important as it relates to them personally. Possibilities are homelessness, poverty, pollution, war, starvation, acid rain, global economy, race relations.

Groups will record how each person in the group rated each of the issues by placing an X on the scattergram in the cell represented by the coordinates. They are to use the horizontal axis for the number of the issue and the vertical axis for the rating of its importance to them. Groups then decide what the scattergram tells them and share the information with the entire class. The teacher may want to make a class scattergram on the overhead projector or chalkboard. Students can turn the scattergram into a graph to help them see different ways to display the same data.

Hands-on Activity | *Paper Bag Puppets Discuss the Solution to a Problem*

Place students into small groups and give them the task of preparing and presenting a skit or mock TV talk show that would explain the essence of the issue that they have chosen or you have assigned. Using lunch-sized brown paper bags, students will create puppets to use in their presentation. Debriefing should always follow such role play or class discussion to find out reactions to the effort.

Focus on Review | *A Hallway of History*

Students choose a hallway with which they are familiar, designate each room for a certain period of history, and then develop a visual image to help remember the room. A sketch should be drawn on the chalkboard or made on a transparency and labels and images agreed upon. These images are identification aides and thus the more grotesque or amusing, the better. When the map is ready, call out bits of factual information and have students point to the room on their hallway map where that bit of data would be placed. Reminder words can be written in if desired.

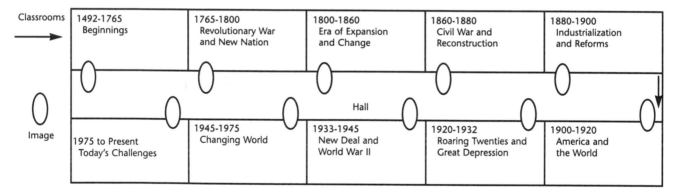

Name _____

Using the Newspaper

Bring a newspaper article on a topic that might affect you directly or indirectly in the future. Glue or staple it to this paper. Answer the questions to see if you can tell what the past might have taught us about this issue.

Glue article here

What is the topic of your article? _____

_____

What basic issue is involved? _____

_____

What solutions to the problem might come to pass? _____

_____

When in the past was there a similar situation? _____

_____

What was the outcome? _____

_____

Could there have been a better solution? _____

_____

Collecting and Using Statistical Data

As an entire class, think about the issues that concern people today as they think about the future. After your class has decided the issues you want to consider, write them in the same order on the lines below. After you have made the list, decide how you personally think each of these issues should be ranked.

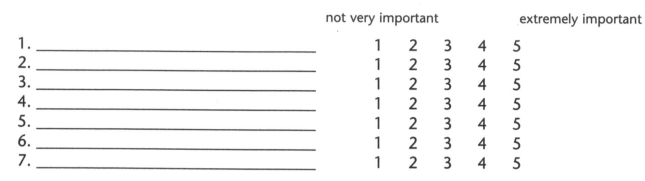

	not very important				extremely important
1. _____	1	2	3	4	5
2. _____	1	2	3	4	5
3. _____	1	2	3	4	5
4. _____	1	2	3	4	5
5. _____	1	2	3	4	5
6. _____	1	2	3	4	5
7. _____	1	2	3	4	5

Record how each person in your group rated each of the issues by placing an x on the scattergram in the cell represented by the coordinates. Use the horizontal axis for the number of the issue and the vertical axis for the rating of its importance. Decide what your scattergram tells you. On another paper, turn the plotting on your scattergram into a graph. Share your group decision with the entire class.

Scattergram

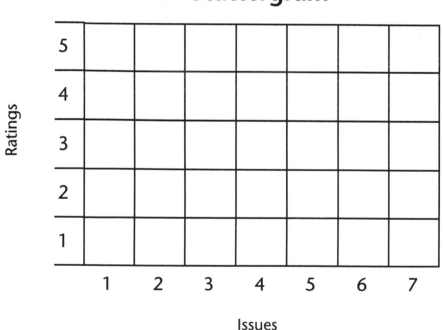

Issues

Paper Bag Puppets
Discuss the Solution to a Problem

Your group has the task of preparing and presenting a skit or mock TV talk show that would explain the essence of one problem that has been in the news recently. Using lunch-sized brown paper bags, create puppets to use in your presentation.

Political Peter

Concerned Connie

Group topic _____

What is the personality of your puppet?

_____

_____

What points does your puppet want to make?

1._____

2._____

3._____

4._____

5._____

6._____

7._____

8._____

Name _____

A Hallway of History

Assume that this is a hallway with which you are familiar. You are going to name each room for an era of U.S. history and then develop a visual image to help remember the room. Close your eyes and get a picture in your mind of a symbolic guardian of this information. Sketch a reminder of the guardian at the entrance to the room. As your teacher calls out information, point to the room on your hallway map where that bit of data would be placed. Write in words as memory aides.

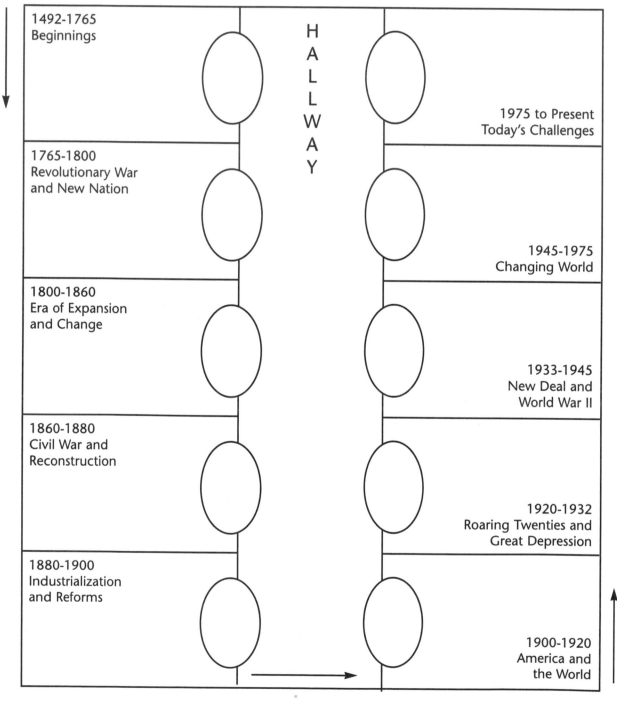

1492-1765
Beginnings

1765-1800
Revolutionary War
and New Nation

1800-1860
Era of Expansion
and Change

1860-1880
Civil War and
Reconstruction

1880-1900
Industrialization
and Reforms

H
A
L
L
W
A
Y

1975 to Present
Today's Challenges

1945-1975
Changing World

1933-1945
New Deal and
World War II

1920-1932
Roaring Twenties and
Great Depression

1900-1920
America and
the World

Answer Key

The Explorers Move Out

Probing for Connections   **page 5**

1. An astrolabe tells the position of the sun and stars. It is used to locate where you are on the earth.
2. The lost colony was located on what is now the outer banks of North Carolina.
3. Oñate set out in 1598 to claim New Mexico for Spain. He founded Sante Fe, which became the capital in 1909.
4. He sailed on at least one trip and decided that he had seen a new continent. A famous geographer then used this first name.
5. They were talking about Buffalo and about cliff dwellings of the Pueblo Indians.

The Explorers Keep Coming   **page 6**

Cabot	1497	England	explored coast of North America
Vespucci	1499-1502	Portugal	explored coast of South America
Ponce de León	1513-1521	Spain	explored Florida
Verrazano	1524	France	found a route to Asia through North America
de Soto	1539-1542	Spain	colonized Florida
Coronado	1540-1542	Spain	looked for gold, discovered Grand Canyon
LaSalle	1669-1682	France	explored Great Lakes and Mississippi

More Than One Trip   **page 7**

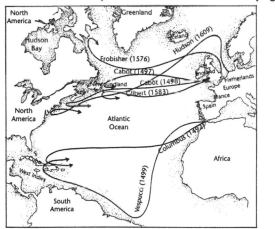

Moving to the New World

Settlement of the Eastern Seaboard   **page 17**

1. A large number of German-speaking Protestants came from Central Europe.
2. In the 1660s rivalry between England and the Netherlands led to a European war. England took over New York from Dutch governor.
3. People had settled in two distinct areas. The north had fewer slaves and grew a lot of tobacco. The south had large rice plantations. In 1712, they divided into two colonies.
4. People who had been imprisoned for debts they couldn't pay.
5. Both colonies were established for religious freedom. Protestants came to Pennsylvania and Catholics to Maryland.
6. People who knew how to farm and build houses and do other practical tasks were more successful as settlers.

They Came to the New World   **page 19**

English Puritans came to Plymouth and Massachusetts Bay Colony to worship as they wished.

Dutch came to New York to establish large estates.

English Quakers and German Protestants came to Pennsylvania for freedom of worship.

English Catholics came to Maryland for freedom of worship.

English came to Jamestown, Virginia in order to obtain land.

Supporters of Charles II came to the Carolinas for land to raise crops.

English debtors came to Georgia to start a new life.

Triangular Trade Sandwich   **page 21**

1. trade among three places
2. sticks of candy
3. sugar cane, rum
4. soul food
5. (Candy will vary.) New England, Africa, the West Indies

Moving Toward Independence

From Colonies to States   **page 27**

New Hampshire: Ethan Allen
New York: Alexander Hamilton
Massachusetts: Samuel Adams, John Adams, Mercy Otis Warren, Anne Hutchinson
Connecticut: Roger Sherman
Pennsylvania: Benjamin Franklin
New Jersey: William Patterson
Maryland: Charles Carroll
Delaware: Thomas McKean
Virginia: George Washington, Thomas Jefferson, James Madison, Patrick Henry
North Carolina: Alexander Martin, William Hooper, Samuel Johnston
South Carolina: Elizabeth Lucas Pinckney, Thomas Pinckney, John Rutledge
Georgia: Nathanael Greene

Moving Toward Democratic Government

Separation of Powers   **page 42**

Executive Branch—highest law enforcement authority; appoint national officials; make treaties with approval of Senate; veto laws considered undesirable

Legislative Branch—make all laws to carry out powers; coin money; maintain army and navy; control spending;

control foreign and interstate commerce; create other federal courts; declare war; make own rules; tax and use money for general welfare; borrow money

    Senate—try impeachments; approve treaties

    House—impeach; originate revenue bills

Judicial Branch—settle disputes between states or between federal government and a state; interpret laws and treaties

Delegation of Powers   page 43

Delegated Powers National Government

regulate interstate and foreign trade; set standard weights and measures; create and maintain armed forces; make copyright and patent laws; establish postal offices; establish foreign policy; create federal courts; coin money; declare war; admit new states

Powers Denied National Government

suspend habeas corpus; punish without a trial

Concurrent Powers

provide for public welfare; build roads; administer criminal justice; charter banks; raise taxes; borrow money

Powers denied to both

ex post facto laws

Reserved Powers of the States

create corporation laws; regulate trade within the state; establish and maintain schools; establish local governments; make laws about marriage and divorce; conduct elections; provide for public safety

Powers Denied the States

keep troops in peace time; make treaties; levy import or export taxes; issue money

Categorizing Your Constitutional Rights   page 46

First—1	Eighth—2
Second—1 or 3	Ninth—3
Third—3	Tenth—3
Fourth—2	Thirteenth—4
Fifth—1 or 2	Fourteenth—2
Sixth—2	Nineteenth—1
Seventh—2	Twenty-sixth—1

The Purpose of the Bill of Rights   page 47

The Bill of Rights does not give Americans rights but rather prevents government from taking away certain basic rights that people already have.

The First Amendment guarantees the basic rights of freedom of religion, freedom of speech, freedom of the press, and freedom to meet in groups.

The next three amendments came out of the colonists' struggle with Great Britain.

They deny government the right to quarter soldiers, to conduct unreasonable searches and seizures, and to forbid an arms-bearing militia.

Amendments five through eight protect citizens who are accused of crimes and are brought to trial.

These amendments give us the right to due process of law, to trial by jury, to refuse to testify against ourselves, to not be tried twice for the same crime, to call witnesses and face accusers, and to have a speedy and public trial.

The last two amendments limit the powers of the federal government to those that are granted in the Constitution.

Because of the rights explained above, citizens of the United States enjoy some very important freedoms.

Moving onto the World Scene

America in Jeopardy Cognitive Map   page 52

Indian Wars—The Indian nations were divided in support for the British and the new country; wars had to be fought.

Impressment—About 10,000 men were taken from American ships and forced to serve in the British navy.

European Colonization—European nations claimed much of the land until Jefferson managed to purchase Louisiana.

National Debt—The federal government had debts from fighting the Revolution. States' debts had to be assumed.

Rivalries—France and England went to war. Burr fought with Hamilton. New England quarreled with the Southern states.

Trouble Spots   page 53

The Panic of 1837   page 56

1. B		5. D	
2. A		6. G	
3. H		7. C	
4. E		8. F	

A Time Line for Mr. Jefferson   page 57

The order is: 1801 Jefferson takes office; February 1803 *Marbury* v. *Madison*; October 1803 Senate ratifies Louisiana Purchase; 1804 Burr kills Hamilton; 1805 Lewis & Clark reach Pacific; 1807 Chesapeake affair; 1808 Nonintercourse Act; 1809 Madison takes office; 1811 War Hawks; 1815 Tripoli treaty.

Movement Toward Reform

American Renaissance—Folders and Cognitive Map   page 62

Literature: Edgar Allan Poe, Harriet Beecher Stowe, Walt Whitman, Ralph Waldo Emerson, Henry David Thoreau

Painting: Shakers, Thomas Cole, Hudson Valley School, Asher Wurand, George Catlin

Women's Concerns: Elizabeth Cady Stanton, Lucretia Mott, Sarah Bagley, Sojourner Truth, Susan B. Anthony

Abolition: Wendell Phillips, Prudence Crandall, Harriet Tubman, William Lloyd Garrison, Grimke sisters

Education: Horace Mann, Margaret Tuller, Emma Hart Willard

American Renaissance—Finding Quiz Answers

1. A
2. D
3. B
4. B
5. D
6. C
7. D
8. B

Who Worked Where

John Deere: Massachusetts to Illinois
Bronson Alcott: Massachusetts to New York
Dorothea Dix: Maine to Washington, D.C.
Angelina Grimke: South Carolina to Pennsylvania
Susan B. Anthony: Massachusetts to New York
Cyrus McCormick: Virginia to Illinois
Harriet Tubman: Maryland to New York

Moving West—the Old Frontier

Classifying Primary Source Artifacts

gold pan	miner	to pan for gold in streams
barbed wire	farmer	to fence in fields
spurs	cowboy	to give ;horse a quick signal
waffle iron	farmer	to make waffles
butter churn	farmer	to make butter
bed warmer	farmer	to warm the bed
pitcher and basin	farmer	to wash up

Manifest Destiny Practice Map

Manifest Destiny Play Dough Map

1. Louisiana Purchase — 1803
2. Lewis and Clark report — 1804
3. Santa Fe Trail — 1821-1843
4. Texas declares independence — 1836
5. John Deere invents steel plow — 1837
6. U.S./Canadian boundary set — 1842
7. Texas annexation — 1845
8. Oregon border set at 49th parallel — 1846
9. Mormons settle Utah — 1847
10. Treaty of Guadalupe Hidalgo — 1848
11. California Gold Rush — 1849
12. Gadsden Purchase — 1853
13. Kansas-Nebraska Act — 1854
14. Colorado Gold Rush — 1859
15. Steel windmill spreads — 1860-1870
16. Homestead Act — 1862
17. Minnesota Sioux leave the state — 1863
18. Chivington massacres Cheyenne — 1864
19. Slaughter of the buffalo — 1865-1866
20. The Long Drive, Chisholm Trail — 1867-1872
21. Black Hills Gold Rush — 1869
22. Glidden patents barbed wire — 1874
23. Sitting Bull unites Plains Indians — 1867
24. Custer at Little Bighorn — 1876
25. Exoduster settlements in Kansas — 1881
26. Sitting Bull surrenders — 1881
27. Great blizzard — 1885
28. Dawes Act assigns land to Indians — 1887
29. Oklahoma land rush — 1889
30. Battle of Wounded Knee — 1890

Moving Toward Restructuring

Reconstruction—A Problem for the States of the Confederacy

Moving Toward Industrialization

Promoting a New Consumerism

Possible answers:

1. human hair, silver gas light chemisettes, elastic waste band, ornate furniture
2. In the past, the ads mainly told that things were available. Now they stress they are better than similar items.
3. They both describe what is for sale and they tell where the store is located. They both have pictures of what they are selling.
4. newspaper sold for 2 cents and 3 cents on Sunday—not $1, men's shoes were $3.50 instead of $60-$100
5. Now the ads seem to be much larger. The writers tell why we ought to buy them. Prices are emphasized.

page 94

	Change Brought About by Industrialization	Reason	Response to Change
Upper Classes	urban growth rich got richer	capital investment owned factories	built mansions on rim of city, lived like royalty filled mansions with artwork, gave large parties
Middle Classes	urban growth mass production more demand for professions people lived closer together	factories needed labor assembly line life was more complex striving for "good life"	had homes on outskirts of the cities people could afford more goods and luxuries worked as doctors, lawyers, office managers, skilled craft people joined clubs, leagues, singing society, charity groups
Lower Classes	immigration to U.S. cities left farm to work in cities need for education and knowledge	to get jobs larger factories a need to know, to improve, to speak English	resentment of immigrants from people who had to accept low pay women and children worked under bad conditions schools, free public libraries, spread yellow journalism

The Labor Movement Begins   page 101

Knights of Labor	American Federation of Labor
Organized in 1869 by the garment cutters of Philadelphia, this group was opposed to strikes.	Samuel Gompers was their practical and businesslike founder and go-getter organizer.
This organization was idealistic—wanted to bring all workers together and give workers a proper share of the wealth they created.	Skilled workers had to belong to a trade union first, for it was a union made up of other unions.
As president, Terence Powderly opposed strikes, fought against child labor, and demanded the eight-hour day.	Orientation was practical, concentrating on higher wages, shorter hours, and improved working conditions.
At first this group was open to skilled workers only but soon came to include women, blacks, and unskilled workers.	This organization charged high dues to establish a strike fund to pay workers who went on strike.
This organization had secret meetings and special handshakes.	These member unions used patriotic symbols and inspiring mottos.
Some members were involved in the Haymarket Riot, which caused the group to be lumped with anarchists and communists in public opinion.	This organization only allowed strikes when there was enough money to hold out long enough to succeed.

Moving into the Twentieth Century
The United States in World War I and After page 107

1. *Lusitania*
   sunk off Ireland 1915, lost 1,198
   Zimmermann
   note sent by foreign minister about U.S.
   Russian Revolution
   Bolsheviks signed armistice 1917
2. Women
   went overseas as nurses, took jobs in factories
   Blacks
   moved north, joined the military
   Farmers
   put 40 million more acres in production
   Businessmen
   increased production and income

3. Airplanes and Dirigibles
   used for first time in warfare
   Tanks
   introduced by Britain, defeated by flame throwers
   Trench warfare
   dug deep across northern and eastern France
   U-boats and Submarine warfare
   struck suddenly without warning
   Poison gas
   tubes of chlorine gas suffocated, mustard gas burned skin
4. Wilson's 14 Points
   Program for World Peace—open diplomacy, freedom of seas, self-determination
   Treaty of Versailles
   Final peace treaty signed in 1919
   Debate on and Signing of the Treaty
   Wilson refused to compromise so it was defeated in the Senate
5. Manners and Morals
   became much freer after the war going into 20s
   Religious Matters and the Law
   There was an attempt to legislate morality
   Prohibition
   18th Amendment against sale of alcoholic beverages
   Woman's Suffrage
   wartime jobs helped get vote in 19th Amendment in 1920
   Women in New Roles
   entered politics, became doctors, lawyers, social workers
   Black Renaissance
   Northern migration, "black is beautiful"
6. Archduke Ferdinand
   assassinated in Sarajevo, 1914
   Kaiser Wilhelm
   hereditary head of German Government
   Woodrow Wilson
   President of U.S. during war
   Herbert Hoover
   ran the food administration
   John Pershing
   Commander of American forces
7. Nationalism and Rivalries
   strong feeling for one's own country
   Wartime Powers
   power to fix prices, nationalize industry
   Nations Emerge & Change
   new nations formed at end of war
   Bonds & Debt
   nation sold bonds to pay for war
   Isolationist Sentiment
   kept U.S. out of league of nations
   Social Change
   People's attitudes were changing
   Prosperity & Depression
   for ten years great prosperity and then Black Tuesday

Missouri vs. *Holland*   page 109
1. they need to protect migratory birds
2. to establish a national interest
3. federal game wardens shouldn't interfere with state hunters
4. the residents of the state of Missouri
5. federal government could ignore hunting, but birds might become extinct; state could go along
6. the government's
7. said the treaty made it a federal matter

What Do You Know About World War I?   page 111
1. B   6. B
2. A   7. C
3. A   8. B
4. B   9. A
5. D

Movements of the 1920s and 1930s
The Arts Live On   page 117
Students might identify the figures as some of these people and then write their accomplishment on the line.

Poets	Editor
Langston Hughes	W. E. B. DuBois
Countee Cullen	**Sculptors**
James Welden	Meta Warrick
Writers	**Musicians**
Jean Toomer	Louis Armstorng
Richard Wright	Duke Ellington
Claude McKay	Harry Burleigh
Rudolph Fisher	Nathaniel Dett
Zora Meale Huston	W.C. Handy
Anthologists	**Singers**
Alain Locke	Marian Anderson
Rudolph Fisher	Bessie Smith
Painters	Paul Robeson
Aaron Douglas	Ethel Waters
Laura Wheeler	
Jacob Lawrence	

Categorizing Two Decades   page 118

	The Roaring Twenties 1920s	The Great Depression 1930s
Business	Expansionism. Over-interest in the stockmarket. Continued economic distress on farms. Push to sell products of factories.	Businesses failed or cut back. People out of work or with lower wages. Stagnation. New regulations. Financial failures in Europe.
Daily Life	Life was upbeat. Things were getting easier because of new inventions. Women's skirts rise. Flaming Youth	Life was a struggle. People didn't have enough money for extras. Soup kitchens and employment lines.
Literature Music Art	An interest in music and literature soared. F. Scott Fitzgerald. Harlem Renaissance begins. Jazz age.	Growth of radio and motion pictures continued an interest in the arts. W.P.A. artist support.
Workers	New jobs were being created because of new products. Assembly line.	Too many people out of work. Sitdown strikes. Social Security started. Hunger marches. P.W.A. and W.P.A. put people to work.
Politics	Return to normalcy after WWI. Kellogg Briand Pact. Labor unions expand.	Deficit spending to pay for New Deal measures. Isolationist mood. Neutrality Acts. High tariffs.
Social Issues	Prohibition brought a lack of compliance with laws. Fear of foreigners. Rise of new Klan	Minorities sought justice. Despair. Bonus Army. Dust storms. Minority rights. Economic equality.
Famous People	Warren Harding Calving Coolidge Herbert Hoover Charles Linbergh	Franklin and Eleanor Roosevelt, Grant Wood, W. E. B. DuBois, Artists of Black Renaissance, John L. Lewis

United States vs. *Curtiss Wright Export Corp*
                                                            page 122
Problem: Can Congress give the president power to make regulations regarding foreign affairs?
Curtiss Wright View: Congress could not transfer power to the president so that he could issue an embargo because the Constitution divided the powers.
President's view: Congress had given him extensive powers in foreign affairs to keep our nation away from foreign wars.

Allied and Axis Powers During World War II   page 123

Hoover and Roosevelt   page 124
Hoover
son of a blacksmith in Iowa
orphaned, raised by uncle
uncle made a lot of money and so did he
studied mining engineering at Stanford University
traveled the world as a mining entrepreneur
a Quaker who passionately believed in peace
reputation as great humanitarian
Secretary of Commerce
Agricultural Marketing Act in his presidency
emphasized efficiency and worth of individual
with depression lost his reputation
Roosevelt
born in New York to a wealthy family
Episcopalian who married a distant cousin
attended Groton School and Harvard University
worked for a Wall Street law firm.
tall, handsome, athletic, and outgoing
charismatic speaker
Roosevelt was stricken with poliomyelitis in 1921
fought paralysis and became governor of New York
believed in betting advice from informal advisors
liberal and progressive in social ideals
said "the only thing we have to fear is fear itself."
led the nation in wartime, elected to four terms

Tree of Life in the Great Depression page 125

Topics that might appear on leaves:

stock market crash
people out of work
people lost their homes
banks foreclosed on farm mortgages
extreme political beliefs
banks failed, people lost savings
everyone felt insecure
supply of goods exceeded demand
soup kitchens
long unemployment lines
isolationism
migrant workers from Dust Bowl
union organizing
Civilian Conservation Corps camps
Works Progress Administration projects

Moving into a Cold War
People Who Influenced the Postwar World page 130

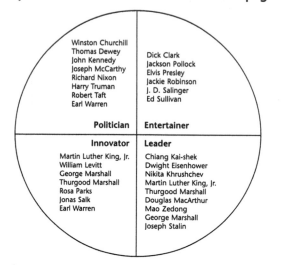

Politician	Entertainer
Winston Churchill Thomas Dewey John Kennedy Joseph McCarthy Richard Nixon Harry Truman Robert Taft Earl Warren	Dick Clark Jackson Pollock Elvis Presley Jackie Robinson J. D. Salinger Ed Sullivan
Innovator	**Leader**
Martin Luther King, Jr. William Levitt George Marshall Thurgood Marshall Rosa Parks Jonas Salk Earl Warren	Chiang Kai-shek Dwight Eisenhower Nikita Khrushchev Martin Luther King, Jr. Thurgood Marshall Douglas MacArthur Mao Zedong George Marshall Joseph Stalin

Contrasting the United States After World War I and World War II page 134

World War I

Returning Veterans—Demobilized veterans received no help. Disabled veterans received pensions.

European nations—United States looked inward, did not care about Europeans' problems. Did not support League of Nations. Asked for reparations.

Labor unions—The labor unions could do little to keep prosperity from coming to an end with the great depression.

Population shifts—People moved back and forth between city and country. New national culture emerged.

Foreign relations—Segregation continued in the South. Harlem Renaissance led to appreciation of African-American entertainers and culture.

World War II

Returning Veterans—Provided for education with G.I Bill. Helped with loans for buying houses.

European nations—Marshall Plan helped European countries rebuild.

Labor Unions—There was a growing economy and demand for workers. Unions helped workers share in prosperity. Taft-Hartley Bill.

Population shifts—People moved to where factories were located. Cars aided in mobility. "Baby Boom" began.

Foreign relations—Communism was feared and aid was slanted toward stopping its growth.

Race relations—Integration in the military and beginning desegregation in schools. Time of the Warren Court.

Time Line of Critical Events From 1945 to 1960
page 132

1945	Roosevelt dies / Truman orders A-Bomb
1946	
1947	Truman Doctrine / Marshall Plan
1948	U.N. recognizes Israel / Berlin Airlift
1949	Communists take over China / Nationalists move to Taiwan
1950	
1951	
1952	
1953	
1954	*Brown v Board of Education* / French leave Indochina / SEATO forms
1955	Rosa Parks protests segregated buses / Montgomery Bus Boycott
1956	Eisenhower starts Interstate Highway system
1957	*Sputnik* / Race for Space begins
1958	NDEA funding for schools
1959	
1960